14/04/15.

D0130351

Please return/renew this item by the last date
above. You can renew on-line at

www.lbhf.gov.uk/libraries

or by phone
0303 123 0035

Hammersmith & Fulham Libraries

By the same author

*An Angel Healed Me: True Stories of
Heavenly Encounters*

*An Angel Called My Name: Inspiring True Stories
from the Other Side*

*An Angel on My Shoulder: Incredible True Stories
from the Other Side*

*Angel Babies: And Other Amazing True Stories
of Guardian Angels*

The Element Encyclopedia of 20,000 Dreams

The Element Encyclopedia of the Psychic World

How to See Your Angels

A Guide to Attracting Heavenly Beings that Heal, Guide and Inspire

THERESA CHEUNG

**SIMON &
SCHUSTER**

London · New York · Sydney · Toronto

A CBS COMPANY

First published in Great Britain by Simon & Schuster UK Ltd, 2010
A CBS COMPANY

3 5 7 9 10 8 6 4 2

Simon & Schuster UK Ltd
1st Floor
222 Gray's Inn Road
London WC1X 8HB

www.simonandschuster.co.uk

Simon & Schuster Australia
Sydney

A CIP catalogue record for this book
is available from the British Library.

ISBN: 978-1-84737-975-7

Typeset by M Rules
Printed and bound by CPI Group (UK) Ltd, Croydon, CR0 4YY

Contents

Acknowledgements

I am indebted to my amazing agent, Clare Hulton, for believing in and making this book happen; my editor, Kerri Sharp, for her sharp vision, insight and encouragement; Martin Bryant and Katherine Stanton, for their skill and detailed attention to the manuscript; and everyone at Simon and Schuster for being so very helpful throughout the entire process of writing this book and getting it ready for publication.

I'd also like to take this opportunity to sincerely thank everyone who has written to me over the years to share their incredible angel stories, or to ask me questions, however tough, or to offer their personal thoughts and insights. I'm deeply grateful to you all because your questions, your experiences and your thoughts are the heart and soul of this book and I have no doubt that your words will bring hope and comfort to all those who read them.

Special thanks to Ray, Robert and Ruthie for their love and patience while I went into exile to complete this project. And last, but by no means least, special thanks to everyone who reads this book. May it open your eyes to the magic and your heart to the wonder that exists within and around you!

Why Can't I See Angels?

*I saw the tracks of angels in the earth: the beauty
of heaven walking by itself on the world.*

Petrarch

There are people who see angels. Of that I have no doubt.
I've been writing about heavenly encounters for many
years now and I continue to be astonished and delighted
by the vast numbers of letters and emails I receive from
people who have seen angels and had their lives transformed, healed, or even saved as a result. It's a huge
honour and joy for me to collect these accounts together
in a book so that others can read these inspiring and
reassuring true stories.

However, alongside incredible stories of heavenly
encounters, I also receive many letters and emails from
people who are drawn to the idea of angels, but cannot
imagine what it is like to actually see one. They often ask

me why it is they can't see evidence of divine beings, or if they are doing something wrong. For some, not being able to see or hear their angels is a cause for much regret, while for others it is proof that they simply don't exist. I do my best to reply to anyone who gets in touch with me to ask questions or express doubts, but I often feel that my response is too brief and inadequate and that is why at this stage in my angel-writing career I felt I should write a book dedicated to welcoming angels into your life. Although I hope it will be a source of spiritual nourishment for those who believe they have actually seen angels, I have written it chiefly for those who don't think they have seen them, yet. Its aim is simple: to give a basic understanding of angels and show how anyone, regardless of whether they have psychic gifts or not, can see them.

Through a Glass Darkly

I can't believe my good fortune to write a book I wish had been written twenty-five years ago when I longed desperately to see a manifestation of heaven on earth, but however hard I tried, I never could. Those who have read some of my previous books will know that spiritually I was quite a late developer. It wasn't really until I was in my late thirties/early forties that I began to see angels. Before that I had a lot of growing up to do.

Much to my regret, I wasn't one of those children who saw dead people in supermarkets or figures shrouded in light by my bedside or orbs glowing in the playground. It was a source of huge frustration because I was born into a family of psychics and spiritualists and when I was growing up talk of seeing spirits was commonplace. If anyone was going to have psychic powers it should have been me.

My Great-aunt Rose was a medium and my grandmother, mother and brother were all born with the gift. They could see and hear things I couldn't. I longed to be like them. I too wanted to see something mystical and magical so I could inspire or comfort others with my visions. My mum would tell me that seeing a plant or tree grow from a seed, or a mother hold her baby for the first time was pretty mystical and magical, but in my mind it wasn't; it just couldn't feel the same as seeing an actual angel, just once. This was something I prayed and longed for with all my heart, but however hard I tried it was like bashing my head against a brick wall. I saw and heard absolutely nothing.

As my mother was a psychic counsellor who saw and heard angels all her life, I never doubted that heavenly helpers were close by me, because this was what I was taught to believe from as early as I can remember. I didn't have any personal 'proof', just anecdotal stories from those I loved and trusted, but this lack of evidence didn't stop me believing that celestial beings watch over us from the other side, and that each one of us has a guardian angel that walks with us through the journey of our lives. I also believed that angels can appear or express themselves through the spirits of departed loved ones. It wasn't that I needed proof to confirm my belief – I just longed to see them. I wanted to feel their magic in my life.

Inspired by the 'knowledge is power' mantra, my first approach was to study, learn and gather information. I spent much of my teens and early twenties reading every book I could on the subject of angels, ESP, witchcraft and psychic awareness. I became something of a walking encyclopedia of the psychic world, and even used my studies to do some numerology and tarot readings at psychic fairs. Later when I managed to get a place at university I impressed my friends, and even my professors, with my detailed knowledge of matters esoteric, but despite all this I was acutely aware that I hadn't had any blinding insights of my own. I hadn't inherited the gift. I wasn't seeing angels.

Although my mother told me to be patient, and give myself time to grow and find out who I really was, deep down I felt I was letting her and my family down in some way. I signed up for a number of psychic classes and workshops. They were all fascinating, and I met some great people, but I always felt like an imposter. I'd get terribly nervous whenever we were asked to do psychic development exercises. If I was paired up with someone else my partner always seemed more advanced in psychic matters than me. They could 'read' me, but I was hopeless at 'reading' them. In group discussions I would listen with awe when everyone talked about seeing auras or bright lights, or sensing information about a person or object used in an exercise. I'm ashamed to admit that sometimes when it came to my turn to contribute I would make things up so as not to draw attention to my lack of ability. If people said they saw orbs or angels I would say I saw them too. In the meditation exercises I was equally hopeless. I had to fight the urge to fall asleep and when it came to doing guided visualization exercises, the only pictures my mind seemed capable of creating were of cups of coffee and bars of chocolate. I never made it to sunny beaches, ancient libraries or lush green forests. After attending no less than five courses, and passing two with flying colours, I was still getting nowhere.

On one occasion I plucked up the courage to consult my tutor at the College of Psychic Studies in Kensington, London, and tell him the truth about my progress, or lack of it. He didn't seem concerned at all, and simply told me that I shouldn't worry too much, as everyone developed at their own pace. I needed to relax and wait for inspiration. It would come when I was ready. I did not agree with him. I was a child of the eighties and ingrained in me was the belief that if you worked hard enough and wanted something enough you could get it. In addition, I'd always been a very disciplined and stubborn person; relaxing was something I didn't believe in, and couldn't do very well.

For the next ten or so years I kept on trying so very hard to see, hear and feel angels. Sometimes there were glimpses of progress; I'd feel so close, but it was one step forward and four steps back. At times I would become very disillusioned and despondent. This was especially the case when my mum died. I'd been closer to her than anyone else, so when she didn't come through to reassure me from the world of spirit, I was ready to write myself off as a lost cause.

I was in my mid-twenties when my mum died and until then I never knew how it felt to lose a loved one. When I was at school I remember witnessing the intense grief of my best friend who lost her father at the age of fourteen. At the time I tried to offer her comfort in the only way I knew how. I told her what I had read about near-death experiences and the afterlife. I told her all I had learned from my mother about the spirits of lost loved ones watching over us. I said that her father was in a better place and she should be happy for him. I couldn't understand why none of my words seemed to offer much comfort. It hurt me deeply when on one occasion I called round to spend some time with her and she didn't want to see me. In my youthful arrogance I felt that I could really offer her comfort and reassurance. Why didn't she want me around?

Before Mum died, although I wasn't making any progress in seeing or hearing angels or spirits, I never lost my belief that the afterlife is a reality. Many times when I attended spiritualist meetings, I saw those who had lost loved ones being comforted by messages channelled from the other side by mediums. I was convinced that death was not an end but a new beginning. I was confident that should I ever lose a loved one my powerful belief would protect me from the grief and pain I had witnessed in my friend and in others. How wrong I was.

When my mother died the pain was raw and excruciating. For me it was out of this world. I would have given anything for some sign from her that she hadn't gone far away and that she was close by, but I got nothing. I cursed my inability to see or sense her. I felt more like a failure than ever. Why didn't I see her? Why wouldn't the angels reveal themselves to me now when I needed to see them more than ever before? Why couldn't I see a glimpse of heaven in my hour of need?

A period of great disillusionment followed. For the first time I questioned everything about myself and my personal philosophy. I experienced a crisis of belief as never before. Perhaps this life was all there was? Perhaps the afterlife wasn't waiting for us? Perhaps angels simply didn't exist?

I was an expert on all things spiritual, but facing my own personal loss showed me I was woefully ill-equipped to deal with my own experience of death. It was one thing talking to others about the afterlife, but completely different when that belief was tested as never before. I remembered how many times I had tried to comfort not just my school friend who had lost her father, but other people by telling them that intense and prolonged grief after the loss of a loved one, although understandable, might hinder the transition of their loved one on the other side. I realized how impossible, and perhaps even unhelpful, this advice may have been, not to mention unfeeling and harsh. Grief is a natural reaction to the loss of a loved one, and no amount of knowledge about near-death experiences or so-called evidence for an afterlife can really ease the pain.

Looking back, it wasn't until my mother died that my spiritual awakening really began. Everything before that – reading books and the courses – had not prepared me for my real education about the existence of angels and what might happen when we pass over. My journey (for it is still ongoing) would eventually take me to the place I am today, where I have no doubt that angels are real and that our spirits live on after death, but before I could arrive at that place I needed to experience the unbearable grief of personal loss, and the painful journey of self-examination that my mother's death triggered.

In the first few hours, days and weeks after Mum's death I took refuge in my beliefs or what I had been taught. I told myself that Mum was at peace now and entering the most exciting phase of her existence. All those hours I had spent chatting with her about her beliefs in the afterlife and now she was finally in heaven. It was a wonderful transition for her and instead of grieving, I realized I should be celebrating her life. So I smiled and waved to my mum's coffin at her funeral. I didn't shed a tear because I thought this is what she would have wanted me to do. She would want me to rejoice at her 'graduation'.

After the funeral I got very busy sorting out all of Mum's things, donating clothes to charity and deciding what to keep and what to recycle between my brother and myself. In the end I decided to keep only a handful of treasured small items. I told myself I didn't need physical reminders. She was very much alive in my heart. I stored all these possessions under my bed. Friends and colleagues told me I was an inspiration to them. They knew how close I had been to my mum and I seemed to be handling everything so well but then, in the months and years that followed, a strange impulse I couldn't make sense of started to take over. I would cry when people laughed and laugh when people cried. I would find myself saying things that didn't make sense. I'd often get confused about the days of the week, or start a conversation and forget what I was talking about. Bit by bit, the world around me stopped making sense.

I would find myself grabbing the box with Mum's things in it under my bed. I would take everything out. I would arrange them all in a circle around me. I couldn't understand why, but I had this overwhelming need to see or touch some memento of her, a photograph, a letter, her spectacles or anything that made her seem real once more. For reasons that didn't make sense to me I was terrified I might forget what she looked and felt like. I needed to remember. I needed to know she had once been real. I'd stare intently at her remaining possessions and then in those quiet moments when I was alone, painful reality and grief would tear up my heart.

The full extent of my loss overwhelmed me. I shed tears as I had never shed them before, as the brutal and huge impact of my mother's death took over my life. She was gone for ever. I was not going to be able to talk to her, touch her, laugh or cry with her again in this world. My life had changed for ever. I was going to have to live the rest of my physical life without her. I'd sob for hours, before exhaustion took over and then I would fall into a heavy sleep. All the while in my mind and my heart I begged my mother to ease my pain by proving to me that she hadn't gone. All I wanted was some small sign from her that she was still close by, some gentle and healing comfort and reassurance from the other side. All I got was silence.

Worn down by grief and loneliness, and too proud to admit to anyone that I was hurting, eventually and perhaps inevitably, depression took over. Depression, for those lucky enough to escape it, feels like falling or collapsing into an endless tunnel of darkness in excruciating slow motion. For me there was no way forward or out and the only thing that existed in my life was the darkness. I had no energy. Some days even turning my head from one side to another seemed impossible. At times there was no pinpoint of lightness, no shades of grey, only blackness, fear, hopelessness and suffocation in a dark, lightless grave. Even my face began to tell the story of my life. I didn't have enough energy to use the muscles in my face. When I glanced at myself in the mirror I looked dull and blank with unfocused and vacant eyes.

Somehow I did manage to get up and go to work most days and having some kind of structure to my days probably held things together for me. You see, when I was in the company of others, I could hide my pain. At least at work I could go on autopilot, go through the motions and pull through the days. But then there were the days when I couldn't even face that. I would call in sick with some lame excuse and stay at home. I couldn't do anything. I didn't watch television or read. I just sat staring at the clock in my bedroom, wondering why it always seemed to tell the same time.

After several months of this non-life, I began to feel like my spirit was dying, rotting away. I was the living dead. My brother wondered why I couldn't snap out of it, why I couldn't make the decision to engage with my life again. I didn't know why. I did want to get better, but I couldn't. I couldn't.

Then one night my mother visited me, not in spirit form, but in a dream. In my dream she came into my bedroom. She sat on a chair and began tidying up, folding my clothes and putting books and magazines in their proper place. In the dream I was lying on my bed in the bedroom, but Mum didn't seem aware of me. She looked healthy, happy and vital and totally different from how she had been in the last six months of her life when cancer took its toll. The dream was so realistic that when I woke up for a few brief and wonderfully comforting moments I actually believed she hadn't died at all, and any moment I would hear her knock on the door and tell me there was a cup of tea waiting downstairs. The knock, of course, didn't come and soon the pain and hopelessness descended over me again.

Dreaming about Mum, although comforting, wasn't enough for me. I still wanted more. I wanted a glowing vision assuring me she was alive and that death was only a doorway. I wanted to hear uplifting words from her. I needed something tangible, something real, not something vague that could easily be explained away by psychologists and doctors as a product of my grieving mind reaching for any kind of (even temporary) relief from the pain of losing someone I loved. I didn't realize it at the time but this dream was indeed a gift from the afterlife. It was the first of many similar dreams of my mother, and each one of them, without me realizing it, gave me small doses of comfort and the strength I needed to do something positive for myself; even if it was something small, like washing my hair or going for a brisk walk.

After the dreams featuring Mum began I started slowly and steadily to turn a corner. In time, I felt brave enough to get in touch with my doctor, ask for help and move forward with my life. When I became conscious of a gradual improvement, at first I put it down to my own strength of character, rather than gifts from the other side, but again I was wrong. Dreams, along with coincidences and sudden hunches, are often the first and perhaps the gentlest way for angels to reveal themselves to us in the physical world. They are also the form of communication that is least likely to alarm or unsettle us. I was in a fragile, emotional state and that is probably why my mother chose dreams as the best way to reach out to me.

Eventually, I did pull myself out of the darkness and get back to the business of living. Curiously, considering my disillusionment about my apparent inability to make contact with the other side, my fascination for the psychic world didn't diminish. Instead it grew stronger. At last I came to the conclusion that if I couldn't see angels for myself I would seek out people who did. I would learn from them and be inspired by them. So I started to gather together collections of stories from people who believed their lives had been changed in some way by angels. As I researched, interviewed and wrote up these stories, and turned them into features and then into books – which went on to become surprise best-sellers – I felt a peace and comfort I had not known before. Perhaps it was my destiny to spread the word about angels, even if I didn't have any proof myself, to believe without 'proof'. After all, isn't that the definition of faith?

It wasn't until several years later, when I was in my late thirties and beginning to understand that there aren't instant answers, and we often get what we need in this life and not what we want, that angels truly began to reveal themselves to me. It began when my mother made tangible contact with me. I'd stopped longing and even hoping for real contact when out of the blue Mum came to me in a night vision. It wasn't like any dream I had had of her before; I had an overwhelming sense that my experience was real.

In my vision I was asleep but also aware and for the first time since her death Mum talked to me directly. She was aware of me. I saw her and she saw me. I could touch her. She told me she was watching over me and her advice to me was to take the right path. When I woke up the next morning, it was like a weight had fallen off my shoulders. Everything about this vision had been different from the previous dreams – my mother had been *real* in a spiritual sense. She had visited me and given me a message. She had also brought my angels with her.

Initially, I thought Mum was simply reminding me to follow my heart and be true to myself, as she had always done when she was alive, but the following day things took an astonishing turn and my life changed for ever. I was at a busy junction cursing because I was stuck behind a couple of trucks who like me were turning left, when she appeared again. This time I heard her voice calling my name. I didn't see her, but her presence entered my body and my being and was so powerful I didn't need any of my five senses to know she was there. Again, just as in my night vision, she told me to take the right path. Without hesitation, and not really understanding why, I decided to take a different route from my intended destination and turned right.

Later that evening when I turned on the local news my heart turned cold. If I had turned left, I would almost certainly have been in a crash involving the two trucks I had been stuck behind and the two cars immediately behind them. The crash killed three people and the voice of my mother saved my life that day. I had long given up on proof of an afterlife, but now my mother had given it to me through a night vision and a sudden flash of intuition. At long last, I was seeing and hearing angels, just not in the way I had expected.

It didn't take me long after this turning point to understand that gifts from the world of spirit had been given to me all my life through dreams, hunches and coincidences. I simply hadn't been able to see them for what they really were. It's a very rare occurrence to see angels with their full-blown wings and halos; the great majority of us who do see angels, experience them in subtler but no less spectacular ways. My mum was giving me the greatest spiritual gift, the gift of awareness. Being so strong-willed and obstinate I had needed a crisis of faith to open my eyes and have my belief renewed.

This is not to say that a person needs to experience loss, or the depths of despair and self-doubt, or to narrowly escape death to see angels. Some people, both adults and children, are blessed with natural gifts of discernment and a resilient personality that grows stronger not weaker with a crisis, but for me the only way to learn was through the school of hard knocks. Unable to find the peace and stillness within myself, and unhappy with my life, and my inability to connect with the world of spirit, grief took over and forced me to slow down, to be still.

I had thought depression was my enemy and the answer was to shake it off to get my life back to normal again, but this is just what my angels wouldn't allow me to do. It was transformation or nothing. I needed to mourn the loss of my mum properly. I needed to doubt everything I had ever been taught to believe, so that if I chose to believe in angels, it wasn't because I had been taught to or because I had so-called 'proof', but because my heart had made the decision to believe. I needed to stop trying to imitate or please others, and looking outside myself for answers. Instead I needed to look deep into the darkness of my soul, and discover a new-found self or sense of meaning. The philosopher Albert Camus puts it more beautifully than I ever could: 'In the depth of winter, I found there was in me an invincible summer.'

All those years I had thought that I couldn't see angels but they had always been around me – I just hadn't seen or understood them. And the reasons I had been looking through a glass darkly were an exaggerated sense of my own importance, along with a heavy dose of impatience and fear. My self-absorption and rigid thinking about what being psychic means had limited my progress and I hadn't been able to see beyond myself and my own prejudices. There simply wasn't room in my heart for angels. I had expected my psychic powers to be like a switch I could just 'switch on', once I had the right information or learned the correct techniques. I had not understood that psychic development is really about growth of the whole person and this rarely happens overnight. It is a life-long process of learning to trust your instincts and discovering within yourself courage, patience and humility and this takes time and life experience. It is also about learning to love yourself unconditionally and about letting go of fear – fear of not fitting in, fear of being called odd, fear of not living up to expectations and, above all, fear of what your dreams, hunches and feelings can tell you about yourself.

Until I recognized that fear and self-doubt were stopping me in my tracks, I would never be able to understand or interpret my angel experiences. I needed to trust my angels and let them guide me through this life and the next. To understand that for those with minds open to the possibility of miracles angels are all around us all the time. They are just out of reach, in a parallel dimension.

Once you get in touch with your inner light, in other words believe in yourself, you can see, hear and feel angels in countless invisible and visible ways. On rare occasions they may appear in their traditional form, complete with halo, wings and blinding light, or through the spirits of loved ones who have passed to the other side, but for most of us, myself included, they are far more likely to manifest as a thought, a feeling, a dream, a whisper, a coincidence, a white feather or other astonishing signs. They may also speak to us through children or birds or animals, or through a gust of air, a loving touch, a song on the radio, an uplifting book, a mysterious scent or in other human beings who are consciously or unconsciously guided by those from a spiritual dimension. For those with the right sensory awareness, the possibilities are endless.

As well as learning to understand the different ways angels can appear to us, I also had to overcome my misguided belief that if I could see angels then all the problems in my life would vanish. Time and life experience and the tears I have cried over lost loved ones have taught me that this couldn't be further from the truth. As I write this I'm reminded again of this common misconception about angels being able to wave a magic wand to make all our troubles disappear. When the devastating earthquake in Haiti claimed thousands of innocent lives my email clogged with questions asking me how the angels can allow things like this to happen. I try to explain that angels aren't here to remove tragedy, injustice, pain and violence from the world – they are here to remind us that there is goodness and love in us and beyond us and, if we choose the path of light rather than the path of darkness, this goodness and love is more than a match for the pain and hopelessness all around us.

Sometimes, for reasons we may never understand in this life, the world just isn't fair and bad things happen to good people. Perhaps one day we will fully understand, but while we are on this earth it isn't possible to step back and see the bigger picture. Trying to explain the spiritual in human terms, and why things happen as they do, is beyond the reach of our earthly capabilities. We should seek out the positive in ourselves and others and let our guardian angels help us fly through this life and the next. All we can do is trust and pray. Praying may seem like a small and perhaps insignificant contribution but believing that goodness will prevail, especially when life deals us harsh blows, is one of the most important things anyone can ever do. After all, it is belief that lifts the veil between this life and the next, and it is faith and hope that brings angels and their pure, unselfish love closer to earth.

I'm hoping that recounting my own spiritual development, and some of the many frustrations and doubts I have experienced along the way, will help you get to know me a bit better, and also explain why, after writing a number of angel story books, I felt a book about the practical nature of working with angels had to be written. I have often wondered, and continue to wonder, about many people who, like me all those years ago, long to see, hear and feel angels, but get frustrated and disillusioned when nothing comes through, or they don't seem to be making any progress. I'm hoping this 'how to' guide will not only answer questions, and be a one-stop source of information about angels, but also be a source of inspiration and strength. It is the kind of book you can refer to time and time again when the going gets tough, and doubts and frustrations creep back into your life, and you find yourself wondering why you can't see angels or where your angels seem to have gone.

It is a book to be read by all those who feel they have a passion for spiritual growth, or perhaps a talent for inspiring, healing and helping others, but don't know where to start. It should be of help to those who often feel as if they can't make sense of the world around them or their place in it. Most of all, though, I want it to be read by all those who need to be reminded and reassured that they are divine sparks of life and that their angels are always close by.

How to Use This Book

How to See Your Angels can be read alone or in conjunction with my other angel books, which differ from the practical nature of this book in that they are collections of incredible and inspiring true stories from people who have experienced divine intervention. This book is divided into six parts, all self-contained, and can be read in any order, so feel free to dive into the section that interests you most before reading the others. Before you begin, bear in mind that the information in Parts Three, Four and Five will be punctuated with practical advice about how to see angels and simple suggestions or exercises to help you bring their healing power into your life, while Parts One, Two and Six contain helpful, and hopefully inspiring, information to put everything in context for you. Here's a brief overview of the different parts:

Part One: The Divine History and Sacred Mystery of Angels sets the scene by explaining who the angels are, and what their nature and purpose in this world and the next is. It will also discuss angels in religion, history, art and culture, and outline some well-known angel encounters in history.

Part Two: Angels Today discusses the current surge of interest in angels and how modern science, the Internet and the frenzy of speculation about the year 2012 may have contributed to that phenomenon. It also answers some frequently asked questions about contemporary angel encounters and shares some modern-day stories. Indeed, from this point on, you'll find contemporary angel stories peppered through the book to illustrate various points made. All these stories have been sworn to be true by the people who related them, or sent them to me via email or letter. In some cases, the names and places have been changed to protect identity, but to the best of my knowledge they are all true.

Part Three: How to See Angels explores the countless different ways that angels can reveal themselves to us. You'll learn how to see, hear and feel your angels, and how to recognize and understand the most common heavenly signs or calling cards.

Part Four: Visions in the Night looks at how angels can appear in dreams and the powerful connection between angels and the spirits of departed loved ones.

Part Five: Everyday Miracles explores the different ways our heavenly helpers can assist us in all areas of our lives, whether in health, career, relationships or a sense of fulfilment. It will also discuss children and angels, animals and angels, the phenomenon of aspiring or earthbound angels and whether or not you may be one.

Part Six: Divine Miscellany is an assorted collection of loosely related quotes, poems and inspirations gathered together to help guide, heal and enlighten you.

The book closes with some final words to inspire you and help you stay committed to life in spirit.

However you choose to read this book, in one sitting or dipping in and out, I sincerely hope it will answer any questions you might have about tapping into this wonderful phenomenon, and provide you with the advice, support, and inspiration you need to see your angels readily and clearly.

As you read please don't fall into the trap of thinking that only special people with the 'gift' of clairvoyance can see celestial beings. Anyone, whatever their age, background or education, can catch a glimpse of heaven on earth. Take me, for example, I'm an ordinary fortysomething mother of two – my daughter is ten and my son twelve – and to this day, although extraordinary things have happened to me, and I hope they will continue to happen as nothing gives me more joy and inspiration, I would never describe myself in any way as a psychic, medium or 'angel lady'. I do believe, though, that all of us are born with the ability to see our angels in one way or another if we know how and where to look. And when you do open your eyes, ears and hearts to them they will transform your life, as they have mine.

PART ONE

The Divine History and Sacred Mystery of Angels

Angels guide us to become spiritual people for the pleasure of it . . . because the spiritual life itself has a great deal of beauty and real satisfaction, even pleasure. And this is what the soul needs.

Thomas More

I'm guessing that you already have a good idea about celestial beings, what they are and what you believe about them. However, I'm hoping that this section will give you some insight into *why* you believe what you believe about angels and so fill you with a sense of awe, or at the very least give you pause for thought.

Throughout history in almost every culture, religion and tradition the word angel means 'messenger'. As intriguing as descriptions of the messenger may be, what matters most is *your* response to that message and whether or not *your* life is transformed as a result.

What Is an Angel?

Angels are typically described as spiritual 'beings of light', with a vaguely human form, with wings and a halo. They are said to be beautiful, graceful and awesome to behold because of their divine purity and power and are thought to exist in the invisible spirit realm beyond the boundaries of the natural world as we know it. This supernatural identity goes some way to explaining why seeing or hearing or sensing them can have such a dramatic impact on human lives, exploding rational or scientific beliefs about life and the universe.

What exactly are these mysterious messengers or 'beings of light'? This question has divided people for centuries, and will no doubt continue to do so. Let's begin with the traditional explanation.

The word angel (*malach*) is an ordinary Hebrew word meaning 'messenger'. The same is true in Arabic and Greek and it is the Greek word '*angelos*', also meaning messenger, which is the source for our English word 'angel'. Those with a religious background tend to define angels as celestial messengers of God, the divine creator of everything. For others, angels are conduits of love and goodness, but they are not associated with any particular religion. The uniting theme, however, is that they are messengers.

When the question 'what are angels?' is posed, attention is often focused on what angels are made of, because they are said to be spiritual beings that don't have the same corporeal bodies of humans. According to the Talmud, the central text of mainstream Judaism that dates back to c.200 BC, the essence of angels is 'fire' that travels upward to heaven. Islamic tradition suggests that angels are created from 'light'. From a Christian perspective, St Augustine of Hippo (354–430) argued that angels were created when God said, 'Let there be light.' Angels are 'light' because they share in the light of God and the word 'light' here means not just light that makes things visible, but the light of wisdom and understanding. St Thomas Aquinas (1225–74) argued in his treatise on angels, that they were pure spirits, pure intellect or minds without bodies.

Interesting as the debate about what angels may or may not be made of, it is important to keep in mind that the tradition remains rooted in the concept of them being messengers. According to St Augustine the word angel is the description not of their nature, but of their role or purpose. And over the centuries there have been many different interpretations of the angel phenomenon, but the common theme of manifesting or expressing a divine message is almost always present. Taking this to its logical conclusion there is no reason then why a person, animal, child, feather, cloud or anything else can't be called an angel, if the role taken on is one of a divine messenger from the world of spirit.

What Angels Mean to You

Listed below are some of the most common descriptions from different cultures. The chances are one or more of them will fit your belief system:

Celestial beings that act as messengers between heaven and earth.

Spiritual beings or intermediaries that connect God or a higher power with humankind.

A human being who manifests extraordinary goodness, purity and unselfishness.

A semi-divine being that comes to earth with a message of goodness and sacrifice for the good of others.

A personification of goodness, light and purity.

Winged messengers of God.

Spiritual beings appointed by a higher power to help, guide and protect us in this life and the next.

Beings of light that exist on a higher spiritual plane.

The invisible presence of truth, goodness, love and light in the world.

The invisible presence of truth, goodness, love and light within a person's heart.

I would encourage you to add your own definitions here, because it is one thing to accept the views of others, whether through adherence to a religion or what you have read, yet much more empowering to seek out answers for yourself – to actually engage in what angels mean to you personally, and see what happens for you as a result.

One thing I have learned over the years is that every one of us is wonderfully unique in our perception and understanding – our heavenly guides would have us no other way – and therefore there is no correct or incorrect definition of angels. I believe in the individual nature of divine encounters and that celestial beings can take on forms that are unique to each individual. Each individual's understanding of angels is therefore just as valid as the next person's, because they tend to reveal themselves in the manner that is most understandable to you.

If you were to ask me what I believe angels to be, I would tell you that I believe them to be invisible spiritual beings from a higher realm that can see the inner light within each one of us. Their task is to help us remember our inner light and the divine potential that exists inside us. At certain moments in our lives, when our minds and hearts are open, angels can connect with our inner light to let us know that we are loved and that this world is not all that there is. They look deep into our hearts and see only what is good, focusing only on our inner light. It does not matter whether we believe in them or not, because they believe in us and our potential. And they want nothing more than to bring love and fulfilment into our lives.

I also believe that you don't need any specific training or clairvoyant powers to see angels. You don't need to be religious or saintly in any way. The angels help anyone who calls upon them with an open, trusting heart, regardless of age, background, religion or education.

You may wonder how I can be so sure, so firm in my belief. I'm sure because in addition to my own supernatural experiences, for the last decade or so I have received countless letters and emails from people of all walks of life, including sceptics and non-believers, and all these people have told me they have seen angels, and about the life-transforming experiences they have had. I have no reason to doubt any of these people. In fact, I never fail to be struck by the truth and sincerity of people who send their stories. But all these experiences are subjective, and in no way definitive. I don't claim to have all the answers about what angels are, just an insatiable curiosity to learn more about them.

That's why I believe the first step in understanding the true nature of angels and drawing them closer to you is to open your mind and get curious about them. Don't be content with descriptions handed down to you by others or depictions of the divine you think you ought to believe in. Dig deep within yourself and come up with your own definition. Angels fly close to people with curious and open minds, because these are the people most willing to believe in magical possibilities, in the impossible made possible. In short, open-minded people are those most likely to see heaven all around them.

When we were children we were blessed with natural curiosity. Each day was an exciting adventure filled with wonder and fascination and this is why there is said to be a close bond between children and angels. Sadly, as we grow older and allow doubt and conditioning to take over we tend to lose our curious nature and our ability to see the magic within and around us. Few of us realize that one of the simplest ways to begin seeing angels is to rediscover the childlike curiosity and sense of wonder that is our birthright.

What Do Angels Look Like?

This is a question I'm asked over and over again by people – what do they actually look like?

Since ancient times humans have debated this question. For many the answer is simple: angels have human form, wings and a halo and are typically surrounded by glowing lights. They wear white flowing robes, play harps, live in heaven on clouds and come to earth to guard or guide us. Many of us have been conditioned to think of our heavenly guides in this way because of representations in religious art, but the truth is their appearance can take a variety of shapes and sizes.

Although wings feature powerfully in visionary accounts of heavenly messengers, and several religious sources list certain angels as having wings, wings were not always an essential requirement and in many ancient accounts, divine guidance is expressed through voices, visions, dreams and feelings. Indeed, up until the fourth century artistic depictions of angels did not tend to have wings. It wasn't really until the reign of the Roman Emperor Constantine (272–337 AD) – who made Christianity a state religion – that the familiar image of angels with wings began to appear consistently in Christian art.

Halos did not become closely associated with angels until after the fourth century either. Until then the halo was a symbol of character painted above pagan gods, so halos were probably avoided for this reason. However, when Roman emperors started to have halos painted above their heads as a symbol of their divinity, angels also began to be painted with them.

As far as angels and heavenly harp-playing is concerned, nowhere in ancient Hebrew scriptures, or the
Qur'an, the central text of Islam dating from AD 610, are
angels represented as playing harps. However, in the
New Testament and the Qur'an angels are said to blow
trumpets to announce the end of time and there often
appears to be a link between angels and music. For
example, in several of the Psalms, praise of God is associated with making music (Psalms 148, 81, 33 and 57)
and from the twelfth century onwards angels are shown
playing a variety of instruments – harps, flutes, horns,
even drums.

The light often said to surround angels is a symbol, or
artistic representation of their purity and divinity. From a
psychic point of view it could represent their aura or
astral body. Psychics often talk of subtle energy fields surrounding everyone and everything. The human aura is
described as millions or even billions of separate energy
fields. The angelic energy field would, therefore, appear
enormous and blinding in comparison and perhaps even
have the appearance of feathers.

To welcome angels into your life, one of the first things to
do is stop having preconceived ideas about them and
what you think they might look like. Angels come in
countless different forms. No one angel will look like

another. You will see your angels in the way you need to see them. If you have a strong belief system your angels may well appear in their more traditional form complete with wings and halo, but you may not see them in this way. You may see them as a burst of light, or a cloudy form, or they might appear as a symbol or in your dreams, thoughts and feelings.

To sum up: although angels can temporarily assume a shape that is instinctively recognizable as divine in origin, or sometimes assume human form, they are spiritual beings and therefore far more likely to reveal their presence in subtle ways, ways that are typically unique to the individual experiencing them.

Are Angels Male and Female?

This is another question that often crops up. Even if angels sometimes appear in male or female form – in films they tend to be often played by men (John Travolta, Cary Grant, Nicolas Cage and Denzel Washington have all played angels) and women who are kind-hearted and self-sacrificing by nature are often called angels – our celestial guides do not actually have a gender. They are spiritual beings, different from humans. They don't have physical bodies and are neither male nor female.

I use the words 'he' and 'she' when referring to angels. When I use the masculine gender, it is not because I believe angels to be male, but because I want to highlight the strong protective role they often play in our lives. When I use the feminine gender my aim is to put the spotlight on their beauty, purity and compassion.

Angels in Religion

Before delving into the history of angels, I want to discuss religion because I want to make it clear from the onset that although many people associate angels with religion, they are truly non-denominational.

An enlightening study, produced in 2002 by scholar Emma Heathcote-Jones from the UK, highlighted the great range of people who said they have encountered an angel. Those who came forward included Christians, Muslims and Jews, but 30 per cent gave no religion and 10 per cent said they were atheist or agnostic. Heathcote-Jones's study shows clearly that if you have a religious viewpoint, angels can slot into any belief system, but you can also walk with your heavenly guides if religion is not for you.

Islam, Judaism and Christianity are monotheistic religions – in that they believe in one God – and they all have traditions of celestial beings offering messages of guidance, healing and hope from God to their followers and leaders. Polytheistic religions that believe in many gods don't have angels as such, but they do have celestial beings or messengers with angelic qualities. The point here is that belief in angels is pretty much universal and angels will work with whatever set of beliefs feels right for you. Violence and wrongdoing have been committed in the name of religion over the centuries, but this has never been the case with angels. They don't offend anyone and wars aren't fought over them. They are without prejudice and will help anyone who asks.

Your angels won't affect your free will or lead you away from any belief system you have. This means that even though they know what is best for you, they won't interfere unless you give them permission first. And when you are ready to open up your heart to them they can help you with just about anything. Many people write to me asking if they should bother the angels with their personal concerns – surely there are more important things for them to do – and I write back reminding them that there is no limit to the time, love and capacity of our heavenly helpers. It is their 'job', for want of a better word, to help you and bring what you need to find peace. You can ask them for their loving guidance and help as many times as you like. Talk to them using words, thoughts or prayers from your heart. They love you to call on them. It really doesn't matter how you call on them, only that you do so.

As you'll see below, when I run through the appearance of angels in some of the world's major religions, different belief systems have angels in common.

Founded by the prophets Abraham and Moses, Judaism emerged up to 4,000 years ago in the Middle East. In Judaism an angel is a spiritual messenger in the service of God. Angels play a prominent role in Jewish thought, even though the exact meaning of the word has been subject to many different interpretations. Angels in the Hebrew Old Testament fulfil a number of functions, including conveying messages from God to humans and protecting the Israelites from harm. The Archangel Michael is the guardian angel of the people of Israel, and in recent years there has been a renewed interest in angels within the Jewish community.

In Christian theology angels are believed to be assigned to every person and their mission is to offer guidance and protection from the other side. In the Catholic faith they are repeatedly represented as intermediary spiritual beings and instruments of communication between God and humanity. It is also a point of faith that each person has their own guardian angel who can intercede with God on their behalf.

In the Islamic tradition, belief in angels may have been inherited from Judaism and Christianity. According to doctrine, the prophet Mohammed is carried to heaven by angels where the Archangel Gabriel dictates to him what was to become the message of the Holy Qur'an, which teaches that angels are the medium between heaven and earth. Indeed, belief in angels is one of the six pillars of the Islamic faith and there is a vast hierarchy of angels created from light. Angels in Islam don't just guide and protect humans; according to the sacred prophet Mohammed, 'Every raindrop that falls is accompanied by an angel, for even a raindrop is a manifestation of being.'

Buddhism is based on the teachings of Buddha (Siddhartha Gautama) who was born around 560 BC. Buddhists do not believe in one creator God, but in reincarnation. In other words, through rebirth we learn to let go of our desires and attachments and eventually obtain nirvana or enlightenment. In the Buddhist tradition, the equivalent of angels are bodhisattvas or enlightened ones who have postponed enlightenment so that they can help others find enlightenment. Bodhisattvas can reveal themselves to people as forms of light or through meditation.

Hinduism originated some 3,000 years ago, perhaps earlier. Hindus believe in a universal God, the creator and transformer of everything, called Brahma and all other deities, such as Vishnu the preserver and Shiva the destroyer, are aspects of Brahman, which is the external reality. Brahman manifests in the human spirit as Atman, or the soul. There may not be any actual references to angels in Hinduism, but there are spirits who sound remarkably familiar such as *devas* or 'shining ones', who can appear before humans as light emanations to help them on their spiritual journeys.

In Shamanic cultures mystical birds resembling angels travel from this world to the next in search of a person's soul fragment. In the spiritual lore of many of the First Nations in North America there is a mythological thunderbird that carries messages and brings light and can sometimes assume human from. The Lakota people called this creature the *wakinyan*, for the Nootka it is *Kw-Uhnx-Wa*, and for the Kwakiult it is called *Hohoq*. (Townsend, Richard F., *Hero, Hawk, and Open Hand*, Yale University Press, 2004)

Since the 1960s a spiritual movement dubbed as 'New Age' has emerged that could be described as a 'post-establishment religion', in that it seeks meaning not from established religions, but from ancient belief systems, for example Pagan, Celtic or Gnostic spirituality. Again what is fascinating here is that angels remain prominent in post-establishment forms of spirituality as well. This can be seen by the prominent place angels now have in both the 'non-fiction' and 'mind, body, spirit' departments in many bookshops.

Angels in History

Religion teaches us that angels are spiritual messengers that connect humans to the divine, but angels also exist outside established religions. They have always been with us. Their presence on earth has been recorded since ancient times both orally and through the written word, as well as through ceremonies and rituals.

Ancient sources that predate the Hebrew book of Genesis (which may date back to the sixth or seventh century BC) show that angels or divine messengers were already a feature in Sumerian, Babylonian, Assyrian, Persian, Egyptian and Greek writings, and it is certainly possible that Hebrew beliefs concerning angels were inherited from these sources. Hebrew beliefs regarding angels may also have been shared with Christianity and Islam. Over 4,000 years ago in Persia (now Iran) and India, people were reaching out to *devas*, those 'shining ones' or messengers of the divine. The ancient Babylonians also carved images of winged beings to guard their temples and these winged messengers later appeared in Judaism, and then in Christianity and Islam. An ancient Sumerian stone column (dating from *c.*2300 BC) in the temple of E-Nun-makh, in the city formerly known as Ur, depicts a winged being pouring the water of life into the king's cup. Ancient Assyrian writings include the word *kababu* or *kuribu* for winged, protective beings. In Egyptian mythology, the goddess Isis uses her wings to breathe life into her dead husband and her brother Osiris. The ancient Greeks believed in Hermes, the messenger of the gods with wings on his heels. In Roman mythology he was Mercury. The ancient Greeks and Romans also had their *diamones* or spirits who came in good and evil form, the good ones being personal protectors. Other ancient cultures feature winged beings with supernatural powers: the winged creatures with human heads on ancient Etruscan tombs, the Viking *valkyries*, the Persian *fereshta*, and the Hindu *apsaras*.

Perhaps the earliest record in history of winged beings comes from Zoroastrianism, a monotheistic and one of the world's oldest religions started by Zoroaster who lived in Persia sometime between 1500 and 550 BC. Zoroastrianism is significant because of its links to both Eastern and Western spirituality. Zoroaster taught that there was one God of goodness and light and that people were plagued by evil demons and assisted by angels of light.

He believed that humans must make a choice between goodness (angels) and evil (demons).

Another very ancient historical record is, of course, the Bible. In Genesis 18: 1–5, which may be one of the earliest surviving written references we have concerning spirit beings taking human form, God and two angels appear before Abraham as men to announce that Sarah, Abraham's wife, will have a son . . .

And the LORD appeared unto him in the plains of Mamre: and he sat in the tent door in the heat of the day; And he lift up his eyes and looked, and, lo, three men stood by him: and when he saw them, he ran to meet them from the tent door, and bowed himself toward the ground, And said, My LORD, if now I have found favour in thy sight, pass not away, I pray thee, from thy servant: Let a little water, I pray you, be fetched, and wash your feet, and rest yourselves under the tree: And I will fetch a morsel of bread, and comfort ye your hearts; after that ye shall pass on: for therefore are ye come to your servant. And they said, So do, as thou hast said.

In its present written form the story is around 3,000 years old, but it may be even older and part of a cycle of stories about the Jewish people passed down orally.

There are up to three hundred other mentions of angels as messengers from God in the Bible, in both the Old and New Testament. Angels are present during the life of Jesus in the New Testament, from the annunciation of Christ's birth (Luke 1: 26ff) to the ascension into heaven (Matthew 28: 6ff). They often appear as men, but at other times they are not in human form. Sometimes their appearance is described as otherworldly and terrifying to behold, but on other occasions they do not incite fear at all. In physical terms, they are often described as winged and stunningly beautiful because they reflect the glory and perfection of God. Angel voices are also heard singing and praising God in several passages in the Bible.

As we've seen, ancient records of, or references to, angels also appear in Hindu, Buddhist and Islamic religious texts and primitive pagan and tribal cultures, proving that belief in angels is a part of almost everyone's culture. It also proves once again that you do not need to belong to any specific culture or religion to believe in angels.

While it is fascinating to find angel-like figures carved into ancient caves all over the world, and to learn how modern ideas of guardian angels have been incorporated from all these types of spirits, I believe it is even more fascinating to look at the similarities in virtually every culture. Seen in this way, not only is belief in angels like a story that each culture tells to reflect its experiences, it also connects each culture. In other words, *devas, diamones, valkyries, fereshtas, kabirus, apsaras* and *malaika* are all one and the same: celestial beings who act as a bridge between the divine and the human and bring with them a sense of guidance and protection from above.

From these ancient beginnings through to the Middle Ages, and right up until the Enlightenment in the late seventeenth and early eighteenth century, angels were consistently believed to play a key role in religious or spiritual life. Celebrated mystics and writers, such as the Italian poet Dante (1265–1321) and St Thomas Aquinas (1225–74), talked of angelic visions and inspirations. However, once the scientific revolution took place in the seventeenth century, and new ideas about science challenged religion as never before, interest in angels declined with some notable exceptions, such as the Swedish mystic Emanuel Swedenborg (1688–1772) who called spirits of the dead 'angels', and the English poet William Blake (1757–1827) who famously described angel visions and the inspirational role angels played in his writing and art. And in 1830, Joseph Smith of Vermont, in the United States, said he met the angel Moroni while praying in a field, and this angel showed him where to find a book 'written in golden plates'. This book later became the starting point for the Church of Jesus Christ of Latter-day Saints, more commonly known today as the Mormons.

Fast-forwarding to the present day, belief in angels is steadily on the increase again. We may live in a more material age that prides itself on scientific objectivity, but belief in ethereal beings has become both popular and respectable. Many of those who subscribe to the New Age movement believe it is angelically led, through contact with their own guardian angels. The New Age movement is hard to define as it is a free-flowing spiritual transformation that differs from established religions in that it has no prophets, no sacred text, no creed and no membership. It is united simply by a search for personal truth and understanding by developing spirituality.

One of the most convincing arguments for the increase in belief in angels is a widespread hunger for spiritual guidance. Growing numbers of people are looking to their angels for assistance during times of crisis. Typically, modern stories of heavenly encounters can be found in descriptions of mysterious strangers who appear in times of need or crisis and then disappear in an unexplained way. Accounts of spectacular coincidences, dreams, visions or other 'signs' that save or transform lives are also ascribed to the work of angels, as are stories of spirits who come to comfort dying people.

A relatively recent story of heavenly intervention that has become the stuff of legend took place during the First World War:

The Angel of Mons

During the First World War, on 23 August 1914, the British army's first battle took place against the advancing Germans at Mons in Belgium. Within weeks what occurred became legend. Even though they had fought courageously, British troops were forced to retreat from the overwhelming German forces. In the middle of this retreat a strange vision of angels holding back their German pursuers was claimed to occur. It was said that the angels appeared larger than men, with a central angel in bright light, wings extended. The apparition caused the horses of the Germans to become unmanageable and they were forced to withdraw.

Two officers reported to the press that 'a ring of angels' appeared around a contingent of Germans and so the most famous legend of the First World War was born.

Other British troops said that they also had seen 'angels the size of men', which appeared to be in the rearguard of the retreating army. Their reports have been explained away by psychologists as hallucinations, while others have attributed the retreat of the Germans to intense fighting by the British rearguard. Perhaps we will never know what made the Germans waver that day but of one thing we can be sure – whatever happened, it was nothing short of miraculous and it gave the British army, and indeed the rest of the world, some much-needed courage and hope.

Angels in Art

Studying angels in art over the ages is fascinating, because representations have changed over time to reflect different cultural and artistic interpretations of the divine.

As previously mentioned, from the fifth century onwards representations of angels with wings, halos and human forms found their way into religious art. In the Middle Ages, angels are typically shown as men wearing flowing robes, but in the late Middle Ages they begin to look more like youths of great beauty and sensuality. In the fifteenth century, Western artists attempted a more naturalistic style. Jan van Eyck

(1395–1441), for example, dispensed with halos because they detracted from the realism of his work. The sixteenth century brought with it a style of art and architecture called baroque, which was ornate, explicitly religious, and more passionately expressive than the angelic images of Renaissance painters, such as Michelangelo Buonarroti (1475–1564), which reflected the more realistic art of ancient Greece and Rome. A fine example of baroque can be found in *The Ecstasy of Saint Theresa* by Giovanni Bernini (1598–1680). This statue depicts the sixteenth-century nun St Theresa of Avila (1515–82) being pierced through the heart by an angel.

By the eighteenth century, baroque art was succeeded by the domestic rococo style. Rococo angels became ornate and chubby little cherubs and, for a while, they all but lost their spiritual meaning. However, things changed in the nineteenth century, the romantic period, when celestial beings evolved into beautiful female figures, unearthly and fragile.

At this point, you may want to check out this brief snapshot of famous angel paintings either online or in your library to see what feelings they inspire. Great art can reflect beauty, truth, love and light and make us, just for a moment, forget who we are, so we can remember something better. It can fill us with a sense of wonder and magic and by doing so bring us closer to the angels. Here are some of the most famous ones to get you started:

Angel Announcing the Death of Our Lord to Mary, Duccio di Buoninsegna (1255–1318)

Annunciation: The Angel Gabriel Sent by God, Giotto di Bondone (1267–1337)

The Angel of the Annunciation, Simone Martini (1284–1344)

The Virgin and Child with Angels, Masaccio (1401–28)

Annunciation, Leonardo da Vinci (1452–1519)

Sistine Madonna, Raphael (1483–1520)

Angel Holding a Candelabra, Michelangelo Buonarroti (1475–1564)

St Matthew and the Angel, Michelangelo Caravaggio (1571–1610)

The Madonna and Child with Two Musical Angels, Anthony Van Dyck (1599–1641)

Abraham Entertaining the Angels, Rembrandt van Rijn (1606–69)

Four Angels, Bartolomé Esteban Murillo (1617–82)

The Three Angels Appearing to Abraham, Giovanni Battista Tiepolo (1696–1770)

Angels Playing Violin, William-Adolphe Bouguereau (1825–1905)

If you're looking for more modern representations the field is wide open for you to explore. With interest in angels growing every day, angel pictures and memorabilia have never been easier to find. The next time you're in the area take a moment to marvel at the massive contemporary steel structure that is the *Angel of the North*. Designed by Antony Gormley and located in Gateshead, England, overlooking the A1 and A167 roads into Tyneside and the East Coast Main Line rail route, it is, as the name suggests, a steel structure of an angel standing 20 metres tall with wings 54 metres across, making it wider than the height of the Statue of Liberty. Erected in February 1998, the wings are angled to create a sense of embrace. Even though the structure has no facial features, no halo, and has wings for arms, it is instantly recognizable as an angel, suggesting perhaps a move from the naturalistic representation of the divine to the symbolic.

Like angels themselves, great art is rare, but artistic expression of angels is not limited to drawing, painting and sculpture. Celestial beings have also been written about in music and song. Run 'angels in song' through a search engine on a computer and you'll find that a huge listing of all kinds of music – from classical to rock, country to ballad – will come up. Perhaps the most well-known relevant single in recent years is 'Angels' written by Robbie

Williams and Ray Hefferman. Williams's song was first released to massive worldwide success in 1997, but it has never gone out of fashion and to this day remains one of the most popular songs for both karaoke and funerals, reflecting once again the all-encompassing nature of angels.

As for film, it's not surprising when you consider that angels are cross-cultural, that the world of film has been touched by their mystery, since movies reflect our preoccupations and dreams. One of the most inspiring and unforgettable has to be *It's a Wonderful Life* (1946). George Bailey, played by James Stewart, wants to kill himself because he can't account for money suddenly missing from his business. His unlikely saviour is chubby Clarence Oddbody, an angel who has been waiting two hundred years to earn his wings. I, for one, will never forget the moment Clarence gets his wings, and even though the film is clichéd and over sixty years old it still resonates so powerfully. Then there are also *Heaven Can Wait* (1978), *Always* (1989), *Michael* (1996), *A Life Less Ordinary* (1997), *City of Angels* and *What Dreams May Come* (both 1998) – just a handful of movies in which angels play their part. And is not *Superman* (1978 and 2006) – along with other movie superheroes, like *Spiderman* (2002, 2004 and 2007) and *Batman* (2005 and 2008) – an archetype of the guardian angel? A being with superhuman powers whose identity is uncertain, but who works for the forces of justice and goodness?

If you have a favourite angel story or work of art that you think could help inspire others, please do get in touch with me and let me know. I'd love to create a top 20 list of recommended inspiring reads or works of art created by my readers.

Angelic Realms

Over the centuries many scholars, mystics and writers have felt the need to develop theories about the hierarchy of angels. Gregory the Great, the seventh-century pope, for example, announced that there were nine orders of angels and these were: angels, archangels, principalities, powers, virtues, dominions, thrones, cherubim and seraphim, but lists and hierarchies vary depending upon what source you are using.

Personally, I don't feel that angels have a hierarchical nature, because I believe they are simply loving and supportive beings of light found within and around you, but as this book aims to be a one-stop guide, I will outline some common traditions. Once again, it is important for you to relate to your angels in whatever way feels most comfortable. So, if you have a very human and under-standable need to give your angel a name, because you subscribe to a certain set of beliefs, or because having a name makes it easier for you to communicate with them, rest assured that you most certainly have the blessing of your angels.

Guardian Angels

Guardian angels are said to be personally assigned to each one of us when we are born, regardless of faith, character or lifestyle, to guide and protect us and they stay with us throughout our lives and beyond. They have never lived as humans on earth, although they may take on human form briefly as 'incarnated angels'. Whether there is one angel per person, one angel for several per-sons, or several angels for one person, is open to question and a matter of personal belief.

Their purpose is to help us whenever they can. This help may inspire us with a thought that prompts us to take action, or lend us superhuman strength, or give us a hunch or gut feeling that guides us to safety or averts potential disaster. In fact, there are many instances, which are often put down to luck, coincidence or even a miracle, but which have the touch of a hand of light behind them. On other occasions, there may be an unexpected feeling of sudden warmth or comfort, or, in times of sadness or grief, a gentle cloak of feathered wings wrapping softly around you. And sometimes an inexplicable presence is felt – like a sudden rush of air created by the passing by of an 'angel on a mission' at the speed of light, or an invisible kiss, or the sense that someone is standing close behind you.

Our guardian angel journeys with us through this life and the next and, if you believe in reincarnation, through each of our incarnations. They will never leave us, no matter what we do. They know our every thought and feeling. Their task is to bring as much divine light to us as possible, and to inspire us to seek out goodness and positivity in everyone and everything, and to love ourselves unconditionally in the same way they love us. They can comfort us in times of need but sometimes, for reasons we may never understand, our guardian angels must stand back, cry with us and share our pain as we work things out for ourselves. These are the times when we feel alone, the dark moments before the dawn. But even during these dark times our guardian angels are always close by. They can never override our free will or help us if we ignore them. Free will is a sacred gift to us because it allows us to choose the path of goodness voluntarily.

Some people believe that your guardian angel is actually your higher self, or the divine spark within you, but whether you discover your guardian angel within or around you the impact on your spiritual transformation is one and the same.

The Archangels

The archangels are angels of higher rank who oversee the guardian angels. They are mentioned in Christian, Islamic and Hebrew records, most specifically in the Bible and the Qur'an as well as the Kabbalah, a Jewish spiritual doctrine, and other belief systems. While our guardian angels are said to offer us help, support and comfort the archangels are said to be higher in rank because they can see the bigger picture. They are in charge of all that happens on earth and because of this they can help bring a sense of meaning and purpose to your life.

Gabriel, along with Uriel, Michael and Raphael are often said to be the four main archangels, but their names, characteristics and number vary according to the source or what spiritual text you consult.

As previously mentioned, I don't believe that angels arrange themselves according to a hierarchy. However, because they are a prominent feature of many belief systems, I hope the following information about some of the most commonly mentioned archangels will be helpful.

Archangel Gabriel is mentioned several times in the Bible bringing messages of importance to people on earth. In the New Testament, Gabriel appears first in the story of Zechariah and Elizabeth and gives his name without being asked: 'I am Gabriel, who stands in the presence of God; and I was sent to speak to you, and to bring you this good news.' (Luke 1: 19) After this, Gabriel is sent to a young woman called Mary, to announce to her the 'good news' of the birth of Jesus (Luke 1: 26). Bear in mind that Gabriel, known as 'God of strength', appeared not just to the Virgin Mary, but is also said in the Qur'an to have appeared to the prophet Mohammed, so it is clear that the message he brings is both important and non-denominational. He is the herald and the bringer of good news who reveals the hidden plans of God. He is the archetypal messenger and the archangel of communication who can bring hope and intuition to the consciousness of humankind. He can help us understand and find our path and purpose in life.

Archangel Uriel is said to be the angel of wisdom and inspiration. His name means 'God is light'. In the Kabbalah, he is assigned to the 'middle pillar of the tree of life', and in Hebrew sacred texts his role is to bring clarity and illumination to earth.

Archangel Michael's name means, 'he who is God' or 'he who looks like God'. He is mentioned in Jewish, Christian and Islamic scriptures. The meaning of his name is said to be like a battle cry, and he is perhaps the most militant of the archangels, often portrayed with a sword or lance in his hand. His purpose is to protect the weak and vulnerable against evil and to open up our minds to new possibilities. One famous association between Michael and the military is his appearance to the young Joan of Arc (1412–31) but although he is typically portrayed as a warrior he is also linked to healing. Pope Gregory the Great (540–604) was said to have prayed to Michael to save Rome from the plague.

Archangel Raphael means 'God has healed'. His story is told in the Hebrew book of Tobit, which wasn't included in the Bible but did find a place in the appendix of some Protestant Bibles. In this story, Raphael, in the guise of a fellow traveller, drives demons away and heals the life of a man called Tobit, an Israelite of the tribe of Naphtali. There isn't time to outline it here, but the book of Tobit is certainly worth a look, because it is full of romance, drama and lovely details. In Judaism, the book of Tobit is not regarded as sacred scripture but the angel Raphael is popular in Judaism as the archangel in charge of health and healing, both physical and spiritual. He also serves to awaken clarity and beauty within and around us and erase negativity. In Islam, Raphael is not so much associated with healing. His role is to blow the trumpet that will signal the Day of Judgement. For Christians, Raphael is the patron saint of the sick and those who heal the sick.

Archangel Haniel means 'mercy or glory of God' and in Jewish lore Haniel is said to be the archangel of happiness, love and harmony – the beautiful things in life.

Raziel means 'secret of God' and Raziel is the archangel of questions and mysteries we may encounter on our spiritual journeys that inspire us to dig deeper in our search for meaning. Ancient Jewish lore says that Raziel sits so close to the throne of God he hears all the secrets of the universe. The Kabbalah therefore describes Raziel as the embodiment of wisdom and divine insight.

I've only listed a few commonly referred-to archangels above. There are many more that I could have mentioned. I'm not going to list them all here, though, because as I said I don't feel that you should get too dogmatic about angel hierarchy.

For now, just be aware that the archangels are non-denominational and you don't need to belong to any religion to ask for their help. If, however, you feel that you need some healing in a particular area of life, you could direct your focus by asking a particular archangel in charge. Or you can simply ask for them to remain close by your side. They are happy to do so.

Other Angels

In the time I've been writing about angels, I've noticed that a lot of people get confused about the differences between angels, spirits, ghosts, fairies and fallen angels. I hope the following will bring some clarity to these terms. There is some overlap, but here is how I see things.

Angel – a spiritual being – sometimes visible but more likely to be invisible – that acts as a connection to the divine within us, around us and above us.

Fallen angel – you've probably heard stories about fallen angels, those angels that for one reason or another didn't make the grade and fell out of heaven where they fell into the clutches of the devil, or Satan, and became demons or evil entities. In my opinion, there are times in our lives when we all face a clear choice between good and evil, and demons and fallen angels only become real when we choose the latter in preference to the former. But, however far we have strayed from the path of goodness, our angels will never abandon us and we always have the power to return to the light and make our demons disappear. In short, demons and fallen angels are only as real as you allow them to be.

Spirits – the soul or spirit of a person that lives on after a person's death. Angels are therefore not strictly speaking spirits of departed loved ones, because angels have never had a physical life here on earth. They are simply pure beings of love. Sometimes, though, angels will choose to manifest or express themselves through the spirits of departed loved ones and there are strong similarities between angels and spirits. Both angels and spirits can appear in countless different ways, such as hearing a voice, seeing a vision, a magical dream or coincidence, smelling a fragrance, the appearance of a white feather and so on and the messages they bring are ones of love and healing. Therefore throughout this book, and in all my books, I have and will continue to refer to spirits as angels and use the terms interchangeably.

Spirit guide – also referred to as masters, spirit guides are usually the spirits of easily recognized or revered people, such as gurus, saints or prophets, who have lived on earth as human beings. If you belong to a specific religion or group with a loving head or leader, this spirit guide might appear to you. Because spirit guides have lived on earth they have compassion and understanding for your problems, and they are here to guide and help you on your spiritual journey.

Ghosts – the spirit of a dead person, especially one who is said to appear in human likeness and in former habitats, who in contrast to a spirit has not yet passed into the afterlife, or is not yet aware that they have died. Spirits come back to protect and guide us, ghosts do not.

Fairies – a fairy is the name given to a type of mythological being or legendary creature, a form of nature spirit, often described as having magical powers in folklore. They can appear as swirling mists or coloured lights and can help us understand the forces of nature. Sometimes the term is used to describe any magical creature, including mischievous goblins or gnomes: at other times, the term only describes a specific type of nature spirit said to create harmony and abundance on earth. Like angels, fairies have wings, but the two can't really be confused.

Again, bear in mind that these are simply my definitions based on the years I've been researching and writing about angels, and you may well read other definitions elsewhere, or indeed have some of your own. The point is that we are discussing angels as benevolent, spiritual helpers whose love for us is unconditional, and whose function is to help us feel and understand the divine in our everyday lives. Often you will not have any idea of the kind of angel you are seeing or receiving and this is fine. It does not matter who you see, only that you are seeing and what you see touches your heart. In my opinion, if your heart has been touched you have seen an angel.

Angelology

The study of our belief in angels is called 'Angelology', an absorbing subject because it is part of our search for higher meaning. I believe there is a reason why almost every religion and culture has suggested that angels represent the highest form of goodness and love. Angels have been written about and spoken of by some of the greatest prophets, saints, writers and artists throughout history. Songs, poems and movies have been written about them and they have been painted and sculpted and mentioned many times in religious texts. Angels inspire us to be stronger and greater than we ever thought we could be. For those who believe in angels, just the thought of their constant presence in our lives is life transforming.

I've only scratched the surface so far with this brief introduction. If you want to dig deeper, perhaps the best place to start is with the original sources of stories. Some of the references to Jewish scriptures, the New Testament and the Qur'an can be found in the pages of this book, so you may want to look at those. There are also a number of web-based versions of the Bible, the Talmud and the Qur'an, where you can do a search for the word 'angel'. I recommend the following for their ease of reference:

The Blue Letter Bible: www.blueletterbible.org
The Qur'an: www.islamicity.com
The Talmud: www.come-and-hear.com.talmud

For scholarly, but accessible, works on the history of our beliefs in angels through the ages, and their representation in art and literature, there is a list under Further Reading at the back of this book.

One of the reasons many of us struggle to see angels is that it is possible we've been looking in the wrong places. They have been with us all the time but we have been too preoccupied to see them. If, however, we look within our hearts and devote patience and love to understanding the one angel that lives there, it becomes so much easier to understand the mystery of angels and to begin to see them all around us.

Famous Angel Encounters

I'd like to finish this section with some famous angel communications and visions. Visions of angels have figured in the lives of those who have illuminated the world with their gifts – even those who did not themselves necessarily believe in divine intervention. As you read, don't imagine that you have to be a genius, devoutly religious or a person of extraordinary talent to see angels, or that you need a special reason to call upon angels. As I said earlier, anyone can get in touch with angels at any time. Angels, like love, are there for everyone. I'm simply trying to show that reading about some well-known glimpses of heaven on earth will inspire you to believe that you too can live in the presence of mystery and awe.

Some of the following accounts relate to religious figures, but the message they brought to the world and the legacy they leave behind is so much bigger than any one religion. These people all transcended the accident of place and time, not only inspiring people of their own time but continue to inspire us all down the centuries. Even today we can look at their lives and their examples and use them as a source of inspiration for our own spiritual paths.

I also think the stories demonstrate that what is so often considered 'genius' or divine inspiration is often nothing more complicated than the angel within, or the selfless desire to serve or inspire others, acting without fear or self-doubt. I truly believe that this is the real secret of genius.

Joan of Arc (1412–31) – Maid of Heaven

The first name that probably springs to mind for many of us when discussing famous angel encounters is that of Joan of Arc, the Maid of Orleans, a national heroine of France and a Catholic saint. Most of us learned about her in school, but her story is so incredible I think it can be revisited again and again.

Thirteen-year-old Jeanne d'Arc was the youngest of five children. She couldn't read or write and had no military training but this didn't stop her leaving home, travelling several hundred miles and leading an army of unruly soldiers to victory. According to Joan, these incredible feats were possible because her angels spoke to her and gave her the guidance, wisdom and courage she needed. Throughout her short but dramatic and action-packed life Joan never lost faith in her angels, even though many doubted her.

From the age of thirteen she began to have mystic visions and hear voices speaking to her. In time she recognized the voices to be heavenly, naming St Michael and St

Margaret and others as her angelic advisers. When she was sixteen, her voices told her that she needed to meet the French dauphin, Charles, whose troops were losing control of the country to the English. She tried to meet one of Charles's generals, but was rebuffed. Then she received a vision or premonition that the French would be defeated by the English in the town of Orleans. When her prediction came true a few days later the general decided to let her see Charles.

At first Charles doubted whether Joan really spoke to angels, so on their first meeting he decided to test her. He disguised himself and mingled with other men and the women of the court in a room. When Joan entered the room – even though she had never seen Charles or pictures of him before – she recognized him immediately and walked right up to him. He took this as a sign that the angels were guiding Joan and he gave her permission to take up arms.

Before returning to the battlefield, Joan went on to make a series of predictions and all of them came true. She predicted that she would save Orleans and that the king would be crowned in Reims the following summer and that she would be wounded before the battle of Orleans but would recover. Equally remarkable was her transformative effect on the troops, with many giving up gambling, swearing and prostitutes to serve her and their king.

Twelve months later, Joan's angel voices told her that the English would take her prisoner and again her prediction came true. She told her captors that 'within seven years' they would lose something important and six years and eight months later the English lost Paris to the French. Joan, however, never lived to see this prediction come true because soon after her capture, at the tender age of nineteen, she was burned at the stake for heresy. Right until the end she said that her voices came from God and she did not doubt them. According to legend her heart would not burn.

Among the many important figures of history just a few stand out as transcending the events of their time and place and Joan of Arc is one such. Although she is a French national heroine she has also become a heroine to many people all over the world. Although she was a devout Catholic, and five centuries later was finally canonized as St Joan of Arc, she has become an inspiration to people of all faiths – and not just people of faith but atheists and agnostics too. And although born nearly six centuries ago she remains an inspiration to this day with depictions of her in art, literature, music, dance and film.

St Francis of Assisi (1181–1226) – Angel of Peace

St Francis of Assisi is honoured by the Catholic Church as the patron saint of animals, the poor, ecology and peace but, like Joan of Arc, his example transcends his religion.

Born in the small Italian town of Assisi, Giovanni Francesco di Bernardone was born into a life of privilege and luxury. His father was a rich merchant and his mother a noblewoman but in his teenage years he disappointed his parents with his life of drinking and partying. His life of ease came to an abrupt end at the age of nineteen when his country called him to war and he was taken prisoner and held captive for a year. When released a dream told him to return to Assisi and when he did his friends and family noticed how much he had changed. Gone was the selfish young boy; he had transformed into a humble man who chose a life of frugality and prayer.

Soon after returning to Assisi, as he was praying in the deserted and decrepit chapel of St Damian's, Francesco heard a voice, telling him to 'Go, Francis, and repair my house which you see is falling down.' Francis took this to be a divine command and sold his horse and some cloth from his father's house in an effort to raise funds to repair the chapel. Things didn't go according to plan because

Francis's father was furious and the priest refused to accept the money. Terrified of his father, Francis hid in a cave for several weeks but eventually his father found him, beat him and took him before the bishop to disinherit him. Once in front of the bishop Francis made a dramatic statement by taking off all his clothes, handing them to his father and saying that from now on his only father was 'Our father who art in heaven.'

After this Francis had no option but to leave Assisi. He wandered around the countryside from one menial job to another and was beaten and robbed many times. Eventually, he returned to Assisi and started to rebuild the little chapel of St Damian's by hand. He went on to restore two other chapels, which later became the centre of the Franciscan order of monks.

While he was hearing mass at the chapel of St Mary, Francis received the signs from heaven he had been searching for. After hearing the gospel that day, which told how Christ's disciples were to have few possessions and no money, he opened the book of the Gospels at random three times in a row and each time it opened at passages where Christ told his disciples to renounce all material possessions and follow him. From then on this became the rule of life for both Francis and his followers. He gave away all his possessions to the poor, put on a brown peasant's cloak and tied a rope around his waist and began to preach the gospel of peace and love.

Inspired by Francis, and encouraged by a dream in which he saw the 'poor man of Assisi', Pope Innocent III gave Francis and his monks permission to preach wherever they liked. From then on Francis devoted his life to preaching the gospel of love and peace throughout Spain and Italy. Typically preaching outside to admiring crowds who serenaded him with music, Francis did not just teach the message of love for other people, he taught the message of love for animals, birds, plants, trees, flowers, stars and all of creation. Many legends tell how animals and birds and insects would mingle among the crowds and listen to his words.

Although Francis had received dreams and other signs from heaven it was not until he was forty-four that an angel actually appeared to him. He and his followers had climbed a mountain behind Assisi to pray and he had a vision of an angel playing a violin. The note the angel played was so lovely that Francis's heart felt as if it would burst with joy. A few nights later, Francis had a vision of an angel again, and villagers living below the mountain saw a bright light near where Francis and his followers were praying.

Soon after, the years of hardship caught up with him and Francis fell ill and became almost blind. Before he died on

3 October 1226, in his beloved St Mary's chapel, he composed one of the most memorable and lovely poems ever written in Italian, 'The Canticle of the Sun'. He was canonized by Pope Gregory IX, a year after his death.

Francis called for simplicity of life, poverty, and humility. He saw heaven in everything and everyone. He worked to care for the poor, and one of his first actions after his conversion was to care for lepers. Thousands were drawn to his sincerity, piety and joy. In many ways a mystic, Francis viewed all nature as a mirror of the divine, calling all creatures his brothers and sisters. In 1212, he allowed the formation of an order for women, called the Poor Clares. Probably no saint has affected so many people as the gentle saint of Assisi who devoted his life to the poor and the sick, preaching a gospel of kindness and love.

Emanuel Swedenborg (1688–1772) – Walking with Angels

Like St Francis of Assisi, Emanuel Swedenborg was born into a life of privilege and ease and then underwent a dramatic transformation.

Born in Stockholm to a father who was a wealthy Lutheran bishop, he trained as a scientist and was noted for his work in the field of astronomy where he developed a theory to explain the creation of the planets. He was also something of an inventor and produced plans for a prototype submarine way ahead of its time. His intelligence impressed King Charles XII of Sweden and through the king's influence Swedenborg later became Professor of Theology at Uppsala University and Bishop of Skara. He could easily have stayed in his respected position until he retired but in 1746, when he was fifty-seven, Swedenborg dramatically resigned and made a great U-turn by announcing that he had become a visionary and mystic.

About three years before he resigned he had begun to experience dreams and visions of heaven and its wonders. He claimed he had been granted the gift of clairvoyance of future events and could speak to the angels and spirits. Eventually, he would go on to define his entire life as one lived among the angels.

He believed he was a divine messenger and his purpose was to disseminate his revelations to others, recording his visions in many books, including *On Heaven and its Wonder and Hell*, and went on to exert a huge influence over writers and artists, including William Blake, Goethe and Dostoyevsky.

Swedenborg taught that God created man to exist in both the physical and spiritual worlds. The spiritual world is an inner vision that most people struggle to make contact with, but it is this inner world that survives death with its own memory of life intact. God can only be revealed through each one of us, and all have the freedom to live lives of goodness or evil. Swedenborg also taught that heaven and angelic guidance is for people of all religions, not just Christians. In heaven there is only love and goodness, whereas in hell there is only hate and pain.

He believed that because our inner world is spiritual, we are all actually angels in heaven. This means that we are in a community of angels while living in our physical body, even if we are not aware of it, and after we are released from our physical bodies by death we associate with angels. In other words, angels exist within us and all around us in this life and the next. Many of his peers thought that his belief in angels and views on the afterlife were misguided, but his visions went on to influence millions. After his death in 1772, a Swedenborg movement founded the New Jerusalem Church and later the Swedenborg Society, which still flourishes today.

William Blake (1757–1827) – Visions of Heaven

Buried in a pauper's grave, and his artistry neglected by his own generation, Blake is now considered a seminal and influential figure in both literature and the visual arts. According to Blake, it was his visions of angels that inspired his achievements and he had his first vision in 1767, when at the age of ten he saw angels on a tree. After that he went on to have numerous other angel encounters and allegedly communicated with spirits of the dead.

Blake's parents encouraged his mystic visions and even though they had little money they helped him to become a painter. Even so, Blake eventually decided to train as an engraver, a profession more likely to generate an income. When he was thirty, he revolutionized the art of engraving by developing a technique called 'illuminated painting' that he said had been revealed to him by his departed brother, Robert, in a vision. This new method allowed Blake to engrave both pictures and handwriting on one metal plate, thus reducing the cost of printing and enhancing the quality of the engraving. For the first time words and pictures could now appear together on the same page and Blake went on to not only illustrate his own writing but also other classics, such as Dante's *Divine Comedy*.

Even though he did not have much recognition in his lifetime and rejected conventional religion, Blake had the help of his angels and his legacy in both art and poetry will never be forgotten. He is probably best remembered as a poet and wrote some of the best-known poems in the English language in his two books: *Songs of Innocence* and *Songs of Experience*, including 'The Tyger' – ('Tyger! Tyger! burning bright'). In other works he wrote 'Jerusalem' as well as this less well-known but beautiful poem called 'The Angel that presided o'er my birth':

> *The Angel that presided o'er my birth*
> *Said, 'Little creature, form'd of Joy and Mirth,*
> *Go love without the help of any Thing on Earth.'*

A truly creative and loving soul, neglected and misunderstood by the world, but appreciated by an elect few, Blake led a contented life of poverty illuminated by visions and angelic inspirations. Perhaps his life is summed up by his lines in 'Auguries of Innocence' that innocence and joy is:

> *To see a world in a grain of sand,*
> *And a heaven in a wild flower,*
> *Hold infinity in the palm of your hand,*
> *And eternity in an hour.*

In my angel books I often find myself referencing Blake's unforgettable image of seeing 'a world in a grain of sand',

and 'a heaven in a wild flower', because it describes better than I ever could how we can all 'hold infinity' in the palm of our hand, if we can see the miracle and beauty not just in a grain of sand but in a blade of grass, a wild flower, a bird, a white feather, a cloud, a sunrise, a smile, a song, a hug, or anything else that inspires you or speaks to your heart. In other words, Blake's remarkable words can inspire us to see the universe for what it really is – a place of unexpected wonder where miracles are possible and angels are all around.

George Frederick Handel (1685–1759) – Visionary Composer

Composed in London in 1741 by Handel, the *Messiah* is considered to be one of the greatest inspirational works in the history of music, but what many of us may not realize is that it was inspired by angels.

Handel grew up in Germany but settled in England in 1712. By the time he was thirty he was already an accomplished composer, famous throughout Europe and celebrated by royalty and church leaders for his operas and church music. Despite this success and acclaim, his finances were far from certain. In his early fifties Handel had what could have been his first angel experience when he was convalescing at a convent in

France and tried to play the harpsichord with an arm paralysed by a recent stroke. Incredibly, perfect music came from the instrument and Handel believed it was the angels playing for him.

When he returned to London, Handel's fortunes didn't improve. He composed two oratorios and they were poorly received. After these disappointments he was left with only one more commission from a charity in Dublin to support those in a debtors' prison. Inspired by angels, whose divinity he tried to portray in his music, Handel composed the *Messiah* in just three weeks. Perhaps the most famous part of the *Messiah* is the Hallelujah Chorus. One story tells that an assistant walked into Handel's room after shouting to him for several minutes with no response. The assistant reportedly found Handel in tears, and when he asked what was wrong, Handel held up the score to the Hallelujah Chorus and said, 'I thought I saw the face of God.'

The first performance of the *Messiah* took place in Dublin in 1742. Handel did not earn much from it, but the proceeds enabled over a hundred men to be freed from debtors' prison. Other performances of the *Messiah* also went on to earn significant amounts for charity.

Handel died at the age of seventy-four. Even though he was German-born he was buried in Westminster Abbey alongside other great artists and statesmen. His divinely inspired music also includes other well-known works such as *Water Music* and *Music for the Royal Fireworks*, and influenced later composers such as Haydn and Beethoven.

Hildegard of Bingen (1098–1179) – Angel of the Rhine

Hildegard of Bingen was a Christian mystic and writer whose life was marked by twenty-six visions of divinity and light: '. . . Then I saw the lucent sky, in which I heard different kinds of music, marvellously embodying all the meanings I had heard before. I heard the phrases of the joyous citizens of heaven, steadfastly preserving the ways of truth . . .'

Hildegard was born into a noble German family and went on to become a Benedictine abbess. At a time when few women wrote she produced major works of theology and visionary writings. Way ahead of her time, she advised kings, popes and bishops, writing treatises about natural history and the use of plants, animals, trees and stones in medicine.

Hildegard's story is important to all students of medieval history and culture, but it is even more important as an inspirational account of an irrepressible spirit and vibrant intellect overcoming social, physical and gender barriers to inspire the world.

George Washington (1732–99) – Divine Union

George Washington was the commander of the Continental Army in the American Revolutionary War (1775–83) and the first President of the United States of America (1789–97). For his crucial role in the formation of the United States, he is often referred to as the father of his country. Few people today realize that Washington had a vision of his country's future and in that vision an angel spoke to him and revealed to him the destiny of the United States.

Various accounts of Washington's vision exist and although they differ in details they all agree in content. The time was the long, cold winter of 1777 and the place was Valley Forge where Washington had retreated with his troops after numerous defeats by the British army. Morale was low and food was scarce. Here, allegedly in his own words, is Washington's account of his vision, which makes fascinating reading. It is fairly lengthy, but I'm including it here because it is certainly worth a look:

This afternoon, as I was sitting at this table engaged in preparing a dispatch, something seemed to disturb me. Looking up, I beheld standing opposite me a singularly beautiful female. So astonished was I, for I had given strict orders not to be disturbed, that it was some moments before I found language to inquire the cause of her presence. A second, a third and even a fourth time did I repeat my question, but received no answer from my mysterious visitor except a slight raising of her eyes.

By this time I felt strange sensations spreading through me. I would have risen but the riveted gaze of the being before me rendered volition impossible. I assayed once more to address her, but my tongue had become useless, as though it had become paralyzed.

A new influence, mysterious, potent, irresistible, took possession of me. All I could do was to gaze steadily, vacantly at my unknown visitor. Gradually the surrounding atmosphere seemed as if it had become filled with sensations, and luminous. Everything about me seemed to rarify, the mysterious visitor herself becoming more airy and yet more distinct to my sight than before. I now began to feel as one dying, or rather to experience the sensations which I have sometimes imagined accompany dissolution. I did not think, I did not reason, I did not move; all were alike impossible. I was only conscious of gazing fixedly, vacantly at my Companion.

Presently I heard a voice saying, 'Son of the Republic,

look and learn,' while at the same time my visitor extended her arm eastwardly. I now beheld a heavy white vapor at some distance rising fold upon fold. This gradually dissipated, and I looked upon a strange scene. Before me lay spread out in one vast plain all the countries of the world – Europe, Asia, Africa and America. I saw rolling and tossing between Europe and America the billows of the Atlantic, and between Asia and America lay the Pacific.

'Son of the Republic,' said the same mysterious voice as before, 'look and learn.' At that moment I beheld a dark, shadowy being, like an angel, standing, or rather floating in midair; between Europe and America. Dipping water out of the ocean in the hollow of each hand, he sprinkled some upon America with his right hand, while with his left hand he cast some on Europe. Immediately a cloud raised from these countries, and joined in mid-ocean. For a while it remained stationary, and then moved slowly westward, until it enveloped America in its murky folds. Sharp flashes of lightning gleamed through it at intervals, and I heard the smothered groans and cries of the American people.

A second time the angel dipped water from the ocean, and sprinkled it out as before. The dark cloud was then drawn back to the ocean, in whose heaving billows it sank from view. A third time I heard the mysterious voice saying, 'Son of the Republic, look and learn,' I cast my eyes upon America and beheld villages and towns and cities springing up one after another until the whole land from the Atlantic to the Pacific was dotted with them.

Again, I heard the mysterious voice say, 'Son of the Republic, the end of the century cometh, look and learn.' At this the dark shadowy angel turned his face southward, and from Africa I saw an ill-omened spectre approach our land. It flitted slowly over every town and city of the latter. The inhabitants presently set themselves in battle array against each other. As I continued looking I saw a bright angel, on whose brow rested a crown of light, on which was traced the word 'Union', bearing the American flag which he placed between the divided nation, and said, 'Remember ye are brethren.' Instantly, the inhabitants, casting from them their weapons became friends once more, and united around the National Standard.

And again I heard the mysterious voice saying, 'Son of the Republic, look and learn.' At this the dark, shadowy angel placed a trumpet to his mouth, and blew three distinct blasts; and taking water from the ocean, he sprinkled it upon Europe, Asia and Africa. Then my eyes beheld a fearful scene: from each of these countries arose thick, black clouds that were soon joined into one. Throughout this mass there gleamed a dark red light by which I saw hordes of armed men, who, moving with the cloud, marched by land and sailed by sea to America.

Our country was enveloped in this volume of cloud, and I saw these vast armies devastate the whole country and burn the villages, towns and cities that I beheld springing up. As my ears listened to the thundering of the cannon, clashing of swords, and the shouts and cries of millions in mortal combat, I heard again the mysterious voice saying, 'Son of the Republic, look and learn.' When the voice had ceased, the dark shadowy angel placed his trumpet once more to his mouth, and blew a long and fearful blast.

Instantly a light as of a thousand suns shone down from above me, and pierced and broke into fragments the dark cloud which enveloped America. At the same moment the angel upon whose head still shone the word 'Union', and who bore our national flag in one hand and a sword in the other, descended from the heavens attended by legions of white spirits. These immediately joined the inhabitants of America, who I perceived were well nigh overcome, but who immediately taking courage again, closed up their broken ranks and renewed the battle.

Again, amid the fearful noise of the conflict, I heard the mysterious voice saying, 'Son of the Republic, look and learn.' As the voice ceased, the shadowy angel for the last time dipped water from the ocean and sprinkled it upon America. Instantly the dark cloud rolled back, together with the armies it had brought, leaving the inhabitants of the land victorious!

Then once more I beheld the villages, towns and cities springing up where I had seen them before, while the bright angel, planting the azure standard he had brought in the midst of them, cried with a loud voice: 'While the stars remain, and the heavens send down dew upon the earth, so long shall the Union last.' And taking from his brow the crown on which blazoned the word 'Union', he placed it upon the National Standard while the people, kneeling down, said, 'Amen'.

The scene instantly began to fade and dissolve, and I at last saw nothing but the rising, curling vapor I at first beheld. This also disappearing, I found myself once more gazing upon the mysterious visitor, who, in the same voice I had heard before, said, 'Son of the Republic, what you have seen is thus interpreted: Three great perils will come upon the Republic. The most fearful is the third, but in this greatest conflict the whole world united shall not prevail against her. Let every child of the Republic learn to live for his God, his land and the Union.' With these words the vision vanished, and I started from my seat and felt that I had seen a vision wherein had been shown to me the birth, progress, and destiny of the United States.

There is continuing debate about Washington's vision, with some arguing that it has also predicted other conflicts to shake the United States, for example the First and

Second World Wars and even the 9/11 attacks. Whether or not this is the case, all the evidence suggests that Washington was a spiritually minded leader.

J.R.R. Tolkien (1892–1973) – Words of Wonder

One of those rare writers who can transport you to another world with his pen, J.R.R. Tolkien, fictional creator of Middle Earth, was one of the greatest writers and scholars of the twentieth century. Generations of readers, and more recently filmgoers, continue to be enthralled by his most famous creation *The Lord of the Rings*.

Born in 1892, Englishman J.R.R. (John Ronald Reuel) Tolkien was the elder of two brothers who lost their father in childhood. Living near Birmingham, the Tolkiens were so poor they were forced to board with relatives and owned practically nothing. Before Tolkien was a teenager, his mother died as well. He was subsequently taken into the care of a Catholic priest and then sent to live with his aunt and later with a foster parent.

When the First World War broke out in 1914 he was sent to the battlefields. After the Battle of the Somme, he developed trench fever, a serious illness common to front-line soldiers trapped in filthy, lice-infested trenches, and was shipped home to a hospital in Birmingham, where he eventually recovered. But the war left its scar and Tolkien lost many of his friends.

Despite the hardship, Tolkien built a happy home life for himself. He married another orphan – Edith Bratt – and had four children with her: John, Michael, Christopher and Priscilla. One of the greatest gifts he gave his children was the gift of imagination. To keep his children entertained, he began to create stories of wizards, elves, fairies and a strange, underground creature he called a hobbit. The idea for this creature came to him suddenly one day when he was working in his study and thought of the words, 'In a hole in the ground lived a hobbit.' Tolkien wrote down all the stories and they were eventually published as *The Hobbit* in 1937.

When the Second World War came Tolkien's son Christopher was called up to the Royal Air Force. Christopher was perhaps the most frail of Tolkien's four children; a heart condition had made him an invalid for several years in his teens. He was very close to his father and during the war the two corresponded frequently with each other. In their letters they shared their emotions and wrote of their mutual belief in heaven and guardian angels. Although Tolkien was proud of his son's bravery, he was also deeply concerned for his safety and prayed constantly. It was prayer, according to letters written by Tolkien to Christopher, that led him to have an extraordinary vision in November 1944. According to an account by Edmund Hoffman, 'Tolkien's Angel' (www.beliefnet.com), one November afternoon, consumed with anxiety about Christopher, Tolkien caught a glimpse of heaven on earth. In this vision a divine light source connected all human beings to God and each soul had their own guardian angel, which is 'God's very attention itself, personalized'.

Tolkien's vision gave him tremendous comfort until the war finished and his beloved Christopher returned home safely. Father and son continued creating their stories of Middle Earth and in the mid-1950s *The Lord of the Rings* was published and, like *The Hobbit*, it became a world-wide best-seller.

Tolkien never lost sight of the comfort and inspiration the angels gave him that November day. The sense of relief and the awareness that his son was protected and surrounded by light reassured him that God's love is personalized, and for each and for every one of us there is a guardian angel to prove it. Indeed, it could be said from that day on divine inspiration never left him. His books continue to bring joy and magic into the lives of millions of children and adults all over the world.

Charles Lindbergh (1902–74) – Flying High

Lindbergh, Charles Augustus, was an American aviator, who made the first solo non-stop flight across the Atlantic Ocean on 20–21 May 1927. Other pilots had crossed the Atlantic before him, but Lindbergh was the first person to do it alone non-stop. In the later years of his life, he went on to become a prolific prize-winning author, international explorer, inventor, and active environmentalist.

A quarter of a century after his successful solo flight across the Atlantic, Charles Lindbergh told a tale that was equally amazing. He claimed that he had been accompanied on his flight by a host of angels who conversed with him, reassured him and brought him home to safety. The story is recorded in detail in his memoirs and I've taken the liberty of paraphrasing it here.

Early in the morning of 20 May 1927, Lindbergh took off from Roosevelt Field, Long Island, in his plane *Spirit of St Louis*. With crowds watching and waiting for sight of his plane all along the route, he flew north-east along the New England coast towards Newfoundland. Once there he headed east across the Atlantic. By night-fall he was alone in the sky flying across a dark and unforgiving ocean with only a compass, an airspeed indicator, a few sandwiches and bottles of water to accompany him to Paris. Here in his own words, he describes how darkness descended on him and his plane:

Darkness set in about 8:15 and a thin, low fog formed over the sea . . . This fog became thicker and increased in height until within two hours I was just skimming the top of storm clouds at about ten thousand feet. Even at this altitude there was a thick haze through which only the stars directly overhead could be seen. There was no moon and it was very dark.

As time went by Lindbergh knew that he had to stay wide awake and alert, however lonely, cold and exhausted he felt. If he fell asleep the plane would certainly nosedive and crash. Although the isolation and darkness made him think deeply about the nearness of death he didn't feel depressed, afraid or even lonely. Gradually, Lindbergh realized that he was not by himself in the plane and in his book *The Spirit of St Louis* he writes about seeing angels all around him:

Without turning my head, I see them as clearly as though in my normal field of vision. There's no limit to my sight – my skull is one great eye, seeing everywhere at once.

At times, voices come out of the air itself, clear yet far away, travelling through distances that can't be measured by the scale of human miles, familiar voices, conversing and advising on my flight, discussing problems of my navigation, reassuring me, giving me messages of importance unobtainable in ordinary life.

Eventually, Lindbergh spotted fishing boats and the coast of southern Ireland. Soon he was heading towards Paris and the runway of Le Bourget. He had made it and when he touched down he was greeted by cheering crowds. Indeed, the fervour greeting his arrival was not unlike the excitement surrounding the first landing on the moon, four decades later.

Lindbergh went on to achieve worldwide acclaim as the first person to pilot an aeroplane solo across the Atlantic. For many he symbolized the triumph of technology and the human spirit over the earth and the barriers of space, which may explain why it would take some twenty-five years for him to talk openly about his heavenly vision. It seems that as he got older Lindbergh's ambivalence about technology increased, and by the 1960s the man who was once an icon for progress had become a tireless advocate for nature and aboriginal peoples against the invasion of civilization. Perhaps Lindbergh had always carried within himself visions contrary to the onward march of science. Late in life he claimed his ambivalence towards technology began in childhood when his instincts drew him to the farm, but his mind drew him to the laboratory. He also claimed in his memoirs that although the visions he saw on his transatlantic flight 'could easily be explained away through reason but the longer I live, the more limited I believe rationality to be. I have found that the irrational gives man insight he cannot otherwise attain.'

Marc Chagall (1887–1985) – Celestial Artist

Marc Chagall is widely considered to be one of the most successful artists of the twentieth century. He created a unique career in virtually every artistic medium, including painting, book illustration, stained glass, stage design, ceramics, tapestry and fine art prints. Using the medium of stained glass, he produced windows for the cathedrals of Reims and Metz, windows for the United Nations, and the Jerusalem Windows in Israel. He also did large-scale paintings, including the ceiling for the Paris Opéra.

He devoted his life to painting angels and fantasy landscapes and to this day his work continues to inspire and delight people all over the world. In the words of Pablo Picasso: 'When Chagall paints, you do not know if he is asleep or awake. Somewhere or other inside his head, there must be an angel.'

A life devoted to art was not a career choice that Chagall's parents would have chosen for their son. They did not understand or support him and so when he was twenty he ran away from home into rural Russia to St Petersburg. Being a Jew, he couldn't enter the city without a work permit so had to hide, but this did not stop him studying art at the schools in St Petersburg.

According to Chagall it was while he was living in St Petersburg that he was inspired by a vision in which he saw an angel bathed in an unearthly blue light hovering above him. He heard the sound of wings moving and felt a shiver of excitement run down his spine as the angel floated up to the ceiling and then melted away.

Chagall began to try to capture the wonder of what he had seen and the rich blue colour that had permeated the atmosphere in his vision. As the years passed his reputation as an artist grew and by 1930 his work was in great demand. After his wife died in 1944 he painted one of his most stunning pictures, *Blue Concert*, with the faces of his beloved wife and daughter combined with his angel vision. He continued to work right up to his death at the age of ninety-seven. Each of his extraordinary works conveys a richness and depth of otherworldly colour and emotion that is unsurpassed.

John Bosco (1815–88) – Guardian of the Poor

Today John Bosco is remembered as a man who dedicated his life to the service of young people living in desperate poverty in the city of Turin, Italy. To this day, many people continue to be inspired by his example.

Born in 1815 in Becchi, Italy, Bosco came from a poor family, but before he had reached his teens he already knew his life purpose. It had been revealed to him in a dream in which a man and a woman, both of great majesty, instructed him to prepare himself for a great battle. The battle appeared to be on behalf of poor and neglected children. In the dream he was told that he had the skills to conquer the unruliness of these children, save them from the streets, educate them and make them his friends.

After training as a priest John began his work trying to help children living on the streets. Many of them were unwilling to listen to him and he was often robbed and assaulted. Then one evening in the autumn of 1852, while he was feeling particularly despondent he prayed for some help and protection from the muggings. Suddenly, a huge, grey dog appeared behind him and started to walk beside him. The two walked side by side until John arrived home safely. Then it left. A couple of days later when John was in a dangerous area the dog appeared again and once more escorted him home.

This happened on numerous occasions and he decided to call the dog Grigio (grey in Italian). On one occasion he was attacked and the dog appeared out of nowhere and scared the attackers away with its barking. This was to be the first of several occasions when Grigio saved his life and John began to realize that something astonishing was happening. For the next thirty years the devoted Grigio continued to appear and disappear inexplicably whenever John needed protection as he travelled, saving the homeless and establishing a new order of priests, the Salesian Society.

Not only is John Bosco's life inspiring in itself, but his mysterious dog protector shows, once again, how angels can appear in many different forms.

Think About It

This snapshot of famous historical angel visions is by no means a definitive list and, as I said earlier, I've steered clear of angel visions or encounters tied to a specific religion, or those mentioned in revered religious texts such as the Old Testament or the Qur'an, and chosen people whose lives transcend their individual beliefs. My aim was to show you how angels have affected history and inspired certain people to believe in their own greatness, courage and creativity, but now it's time to turn the spotlight back on you.

I'd like to remind you that you don't need to be a revered artist, musician or world leader to be inspired by heaven. Inspiration, like angels, is for everyone. Think about it. Often the primary motivation of artists, musicians, writers, statesmen, engineers, philosophers, poets, teachers and heroes is to simply help, lead, amaze or inspire others. This loving intention is so strong that it allows the angel within them to break free from limitations, fly high and overcome seemingly insurmountable obstacles and problems. Seen in this light all of us are capable of genius, of rising above the ordinary and surmounting obstacles that life throws in our path, if we simply allow ourselves to express, without interference, the loving intentions (or as I like to think of it the angels) that we already have inside ourselves.

Only the human part of us knows limitation. The angels inside and all around us, who are simply waiting for us to see, hear and feel them, know none.

PART TWO

Angels Today

Millions of spiritual creatures walk the earth
Unseen, both when we wake and when we sleep.

John Milton, Paradise Lost

In this section, we'll bring everything up to date by looking at belief in angels today. Sit back and read some modern-day angel stories.

Stories from people who believe they have experienced something magical and mystical will show you how much angel 'visions' can vary. Some see angels complete with full-blown wings and halos with their eyes open, while others see them in their mind's eye. Others see bright lights, or see heaven in their dreams or feel the wings of an angel wrapping around them. Some sense the presence of the divine or see reassuring angel calling cards or signs, such as a white feather or cloud. Each story is both extraordinary and unique and every reader will obtain different insights.

Extraordinary Encounters

In September 2008 a lady called Colleen Banton talked to the press about her belief in miracles. Her story was widely reported in the American media at the time, but for those of you who missed it, here is a brief recap:

Indisputably an Angel

Fourteen-year-old Chelsea had a history of serious health issues. She was born five weeks prematurely with developmental disabilities and had battled serious health problems all her life. She was particularly susceptible to pneumonia and in September 2008 she lay dying of it in a hospital room in Charlotte, North Carolina.

Told that there was no hope for Chelsea, her mother, Colleen, instructed doctors to take her daughter off life support and allow nature to take its course. Then, as she watched her daughter fade away, an image of bright light appeared on a security monitor. Within an hour, Chelsea began a recovery that doctors are at a loss to explain. Colleen believes that the bright light was the image of an angel and that the apparition saved her daughter's life. 'It's a blessing,' she told NBC News. 'It's a miracle.'

Colleen took a picture of the television monitor on which the image appeared. Some who look at it would describe it as a flare of reflected light. Others – including nurses who were on duty at the time – say the three vertical shafts of light are indisputably an angel.

At the time Colleen's story sent the media and scientists into a frenzy of speculation, and even sceptics were forced to reconsider their cynicism after reviewing the undisputed photo evidence. Was Chelsea healed by a visitor from another dimension? I believe that she was.

This next story was also reported in local press at the time. As you'll read, the boy involved has an unshakeable belief that an angel saved his life.

Teen Says an Angel Saved Him

On Friday 23 November 2007, Joshua Kosch was hit by a freight train in downtown Fayetteville and doctors amputated his right leg. Kosch said he saw an angel who helped him survive the accident on Friday.

The nineteen-year-old had gotten dressed up in Victorian attire and was walking to A Dickens Holiday, an annual downtown festival. He stood on one set of railroad tracks near Hay Street, while waiting for a southbound train to pass him on the adjoining tracks. According to his parents he did not hear the northbound train approaching him.

Although the train had slowed to about 20 mph and despite his best efforts, the conductor could not stop the 93-car train in time to avoid hitting Kosch. Kosch said he remembers seeing an angel during the accident. 'He (the angel) told me it wasn't my time,' Kosch said. 'And I couldn't get up. And that's because he held me down.'

Kosch spent several weeks in intensive care at Cape

Fear Valley Medical Center, recovering from rib fractures, broken vertebrae, a broken arm and punctured lung. His right leg was amputated above his knee. His mother, Barbara, said seeing her son survive has been a miracle.

The next story was reported by British national newspapers in January 2009. Perhaps you'll remember reading it?

Saved By the Voice and Hand of an Angel

A British survivor of the New Year's Eve nightclub fire in Bangkok said that an angel dragged him to safety when he was overcome with smoke. Twenty-nine-year-old Alex Wargacki was with seven friends when he saw the fire start in the three-storey Santika club at around 12.30 am on New Year's Day. With the exits blocked by panicking crowds of people Alex was overcome by the smoke and lost consciousness.

The fire went on to kill dozens of people but Alex was not among them. He is quoted as saying: 'I woke up and heard this voice saying, Come on. Come this way. Then I felt myself being dragged towards an exit and then I was out in the open air. Had it not been for this voice with the hand of an angel I would not be alive.' Alex admitted that it was possible a fireman or someone at the club saved him but he can't be sure.

These accounts received a vast amount of press and could well play their part in reviving current interest in angels. It is easy to understand why they have such a potent effect. Stories, like those of Haiti earthquake survivors Emanuel Buteau and little baby Angel, speak directly to our hearts.

Miracles Among the Rubble

Twenty-one-year-old Emanuel Buteau survived ten days under the wreckage of his collapsed apartment building during the Haiti earthquake that killed thousands in January 2010. Speaking with the help of a translator, Buteau told reporters that it was his faith that saved his life. He prayed to God.

Buteau's mother had returned to the collapsed apartment to find his body for burial. Trapped inside, he heard her speak of him in the past tense. He called her name, and she called the rescue team, the same team that saved a little boy and his sister two days earlier. 'If you save one man we say in Hebrew, you save the whole world, and this is one of the main reasons that we are here,' the team's Col. Gili Shenhal said.

The second story concerns a miracle baby appropriately named Angel by his rescuers. He was pulled out of the rubble on the fourth day. He was about four months old. His mother had been killed, and his mother's cousin brought him in. The doctors found nothing but minor cuts

and scrapes around his little body. Angel went on to charm
everyone who talked to him with his beaming smile.

We can never possibly understand why things happen but even in the darkest, most terrifying of events, stories like these show that miracles are still possible and our heavenly guardians haven't forgotten us.

'Miracle' survival, rescue or recovery stories are dramatic but, as inspiring as these stories are, they are not, in my opinion, the backbone of the current revival of interest in angels. Instead, it is the vast number of people from all walks of life who believe that their lives have been touched by miracles, who are giving angels a new lease of life. For some reason, these stories do not hit the headlines but this does not make them any less remarkable.

This intriguing story was sent to me by Kate and what she experienced is powerful testimony that modern-day angels don't always conform to the stereotypical image of having wings and halo. They can also be extremely practical and hands-on.

Invisible Hands

There have been a number of occasions in my life when I
am sure angels have been guiding and inspiring me but

I want to tell you about this one instance when I am convinced an angel actually touched – or to be more specific hit – me.

At the time I was fifteen and boys and music rather than angels were on my mind. I wasn't very health conscious back then. I used to eat a lot of junk food, especially pizza and chocolate. It drove my mum crazy and she was always trying to get me to eat more healthily. She'd nag me constantly to eat more vegetables and would always leave fresh fruit in my bedroom in the hope I'd snack on that instead of crisps.

One evening I was alone in my room, listening to some music and thinking about this boy I was crazy about. My brother was sleeping over at his mate's house and Mum had gone to bed complaining of a headache. I felt sorry for Mum but a part of me was pleased there was no one to tell me to tidy my room or do something useful with my time. I could just chill out in my room. It must have been about midnight when I finally decided to go to sleep. As I got changed into my bed clothes I felt my tummy rumble. Too sleepy to go to the kitchen to get some milk and biscuits, I grabbed one of the apples Mum had left in my room, took a few bites and then fell into bed, stomach first.

No sooner had I hit the pillow when I felt as if I couldn't breathe. I opened my mouth to call Mum but no words came out. A piece of apple had got stuck in my windpipe. I could hear my heart beating and my head felt like it was bursting. I was choking. I could die. Suddenly, I heard my door swing open. I didn't have enough energy to turn my head around and everything was starting to disappear around me. I don't think I heard any footsteps but I felt this hard smack on my back. It was a really hard blow and it made me spit out the apple. Air filled my lungs immediately. I turned around thinking I would see Mum or my brother but the room was empty and the door was still closed. There was no one in my bedroom and the house was quiet.

Shaking with relief, I ran into Mum's bedroom. Mum took a while to wake up but when she finally heard my story she listened with astonishment. She told me that she had been fast asleep and I must have been dreaming. I told her I hadn't been dreaming and showed her the piece of apple I had spat out onto my pillow and how I had not been mistaken – this hand had hit me.

I lifted my bed shirt to point to the place I had been hit and as I did Mum gasped. She told me to take a look over my shoulder in the mirror. I couldn't believe what I saw. I saw the definite mark of a hand on my back, only it didn't look like a normal hand, it seemed to be coming from something much larger.

Over the years I have often thought about that night and it is tremendously comforting to know that an angel *saved me from choking, perhaps to death. The mark faded by the morning, but the memory still lingers and I can recall everything as if it happened yesterday.*

Kate believes an angel saved her life, and who are we to argue otherwise? In much the same way, who are we to disagree with Judith, whose story is below? Like Kate, Judith feels that there is no other possible explanation for her miraculous escape from a road accident. What do you think?

Letting Go

I think the time was about 6.30 in the morning. It was a lovely clear morning and my husband was driving us both to work. We must have been driving for about fifteen minutes when I heard this hissing sound and the car bumped. One of our tyres had blown and my head jerked back. Then it bumped again before hitting a concrete barrier and turning around anticlockwise a number of times.

Mercifully, I was wearing my seat belt and so was my husband so when the car started spinning around we only got a few minor cuts and grazes. As we were spinning I clearly recalled another incident we had had a few years back when we had skidded and spun around on some black ice. On that occasion we hadn't been wearing seat belts and the incident put us both in hospital for close to a week.

Anyway, back to us spinning around after the tyre burst. Things were about to go from bad to worse. When the car stopped spinning we were facing the wrong direction and rush hour traffic was coming straight at us at incredible speed. What was amazing though is that the cars all started to slow down, then separate and calmly drive on either side of us. It was like there was an invisible traffic warden. Not only had we not been hit as we spun around, nobody was hitting us now.

We got out and stood by the side of the road. When the police eventually arrived they said that an angel must have been driving the car for us, because they didn't think that anyone who wasn't a racing car driver trained to cope in such situations could have survived what we survived. Later, my husband told me that when we started spinning around a little voice inside his head told him to let go of the wheel because everything would be fine. He listened to and trusted that voice and let go of the wheel. He also said that he saw my head being bumped while we were spinning but knew I would be fine.

For many people divine intervention appears to be the only explanation for such incredible stories. Here is Susan's compelling story.

Angel Wings

I was driving my car. It was dark and all of a sudden my headlights went out. I could hear a lot of noise and sparking from the engine. I did notice signs on the street saying no stopping or parking so my first instinct was to get out of the car as fast as I could. Then just as I was getting out of the driver's seat I knew it was all over because a large white bus hit my car. I closed my eyes and heard a swishing sound but when I opened them again and looked up I was fine. I could not believe it. For a moment I thought I was dead and I was simply watching the scene unfold. But I wasn't dead. The bus had pulled up alongside of my car and the driver was shouting at me. I think he was shaken up too by what happened because he thought he had killed me. I couldn't say anything to him, I was just in shock.

The noise I heard sounded like angel wings covering me as the bus ran into me. As long as I live I will never forget that night. I was pregnant at the time with my son and it terrifies me to think that I might not only have lost my life but lost him as well.

Here's another breathtaking automobile story from Nick:

How Was That Possible?

Just before Christmas 2009, I had an experience I'd like to share with you. I was driving to my mum-in-law's to get my wife, during ice and snow. The road on her estate was like glass and a car was coming towards me. I was sliding towards it and thought a crash was inevitable. I was waiting for the sound of crunching metal, and in panic tugged at the wheel. Amazingly, I found myself on the side of the road facing the right way. It was as if my car had been placed there. How was that possible? I know I could not have steered it there myself.

Cheryl also believes an angel saved her life:

Leap of Faith

When I was fifteen, I tried to end my life. I don't want to go into all the details, but my brother was abusing me and I had just lost my best friend in a car accident. I walked up to the last level of a car park in Liverpool city centre. I fully intended to jump, but just as I was about to leap off, I saw a lady in a red and black skirt with red and purple wings and a bright light shining around her. She had long, blonde hair. She was standing over the clock tower. She said her name was Julie. She asked me to stay calm and to come down from the car park because my life was still worth living. If I had not seen my angel I would definitely have jumped that day. Julie told me to go to hospital because they would help me. I am so glad I did because I got the help I needed to pull me through this rough path in my life.

I've never seen Julie again but I do feel her around me when I am insecure. She helps me remember that every moment of life is worth living.

Cheryl was only fifteen at the time and, interestingly, I discovered that the meaning of the name 'Julie' is rather fittingly 'youth'.

Arthur believes something miraculous intervened during a time of deep darkness:

Light Years Ahead

Hi, my name is Arthur. I want to tell you about something extraordinary that happened to me. It turned my life around.

In the summer of 2000 I lost my job and my marriage fell apart. I felt like a failure and I got very depressed and morbid. I started drinking. Soon drink was the only thing in my life and the only thing worth getting up for. On the day that my divorce papers came through I tried to numb the pain by going to the off licence and buying wine, beer and gin. I started to stagger home with my heavy bags clinking when this cyclist drove past me and sprayed mud and water all over me. I felt dizzy and lost my balance. Before I knew it I had fallen over and was lying in the street with cans and broken wine bottles everywhere. Cursing, I tried to salvage as much as I could but I cut my fingers and every time I tried to grab a can it slipped out of my hand.

Suddenly, I felt as if something was exploding out of my skull. The feeling was so powerful that I held my head in my hands. I heard this really high-pitched sound in my ears and in the corner of my eye I could see a blinding, bright light that started small and then got bigger and bigger. Although it felt weird, through it all I didn't feel at all frightened. In fact, it felt incredible. The light spread down my body to my heart. I touched my chest and it felt so warm. Then the warmth travelled all around my body and as it did I lost every craving I have ever had for alcohol.

I am in no doubt that an angel changed my life that day. I've been sober these last ten years. I have a new job, new partner and life feels good every day. I just lost my taste for drink that day. It was a miracle. I haven't told this story to many people, just my wife and a few close friends. I'm not sure if they believe me, but every word I'm telling you is true.

Stories about miracles that save lives, like those above, go way beyond trite coincidence. In each case, it does seem as if something extraordinary occurred to lead a person away from death. It's also interesting to note that in many cases the miracle that saved a life was spontaneous. It wasn't something hoped or prayed for. The individuals concerned did not have any inkling of what might happen. But 'something', it seems, did know beforehand; something with knowledge of the future reached out to prevent disaster.

As Mike discovered, sometimes the angels intervene in our lives not to lead us away from potent danger, but to protect the lives of others.

My Worst Nightmare

I'm not afraid of the dark and it takes a lot to creep me out but there was this one advert I saw on the telly that really got to me. If you haven't seen it – it's the one where this guy is trying to go about his normal business, living and working and so on, but he can't stop seeing this dead child lying in a crumpled heap. Nobody else sees the child, just him and it's the first thing he sees in the morning and the last thing he sees at night. Basically, this guy had been speeding and he'd killed a child. I think that would be my worst nightmare. I don't think I could live with myself if I killed a child, because I was doing some-thing stupid or reckless like speeding.

Well, here's what happened to me. I'm convinced an angel saved not just a child's precious life, but me from my worst nightmare. I was driving through some back streets and as usual I was being extremely careful. I wasn't trav-elling a mile over thirty and I was looking around the streets to check for children or animals or people. Then all of a sudden the image of a child lying in the road from the advert flashed into my head. I instantly slowed right down to just ten or so miles an hour. At that point a tod-dler came rushing from a garden into the road and stood right in front of my car. Because I was driving so very slowly I was able to brake in time. If I had still been travelling at thirty miles an hour there is no doubt in my mind I would have hit the child and very probably killed him as he was so small and he just came out of nowhere. There was no way I would have seen him in time.

The child's mum came running from the garden and grabbed her son. She thanked me over and over again for driving so carefully. Someone had forgotten to shut the garden gate. She had only turned her back for a minute and he had rushed out. I didn't tell her that it wasn't just careful driving that had saved her son from injury or death. Her son's life had been saved because that image had come into my head and for no rational reason at all I had slowed right down at exactly the right moment. I *dread to think what would have happened if I hadn't slowed down and I thank my guardian angel every day. Even though I would not have been at fault if harm had come to the child because I was within the speed limit, as I said I don't think I could have lived with myself if a child had lost his or her life because of me.*

Janice also felt the presence of an angel in a different but reassuring way.

Loud and Clear

On 4th July 2007 my mother died from complications related to what should have been routine gall-bladder surgery. I didn't expect my mum to die even though she got sick and was in hospital for five months. I wasn't with her when she died and when I heard the news I remember feeling this urgent need to get some fresh air. I was at home and stepped outside onto my porch. As soon as I was outside I felt my mother all around me as if she was standing in front of me. It's so hard to describe but I just knew she was there.

I looked up and saw the wind chime my mum had given me as a house-warming present. It was a warm day and there was very little breeze but something inside me asked my mum to ring the chime for me. All of a sudden the chime started to ring, loud and clear. It rang like that without any breeze to make it ring for about thirty seconds and then it stopped. It was a beautiful experience and a gift that helped begin to heal my tremendous grief.

Many bereaved people have written to me to say that they see, hear or feel reassuring signs at significant moments. For Janice it was the sound of a wind chime, for Nicola it was an invisible kiss.

One Last Kiss

My mother used to be a nurse and she had seen many dead bodies in her time. She used to tell me that she never wanted me to see her like that. When she died she wanted me to remember her alive and full of vitality and didn't want me to see her body when she had gone. So when the hospital called to say she had died suddenly in the night and asked me if I wanted to see her one more time, I immediately said no.

In the days before the funeral I was under a lot of pressure from friends and family to say my goodbyes. They were all very well meaning and were trying to ease my grief. My husband told me that he had visited his father after he died and it had been incredibly healing for him. I told him that although that may have worked for him it wasn't right for me. Everyone told me that I would regret it but I had made my mind up.

I was firm in my decision right up until an hour or so before the funeral when I started to waver for the first time. A part of me wanted to hold Mum one more time, to kiss her and say goodbye. I wasn't ready. I thought of Mum lying alone in her coffin. Perhaps she needed to be held as much as I longed to hold her. Perhaps I was wrong and everyone was right? Perhaps I needed closure?

I was sitting there feeling wretched when I felt this gust of air on my cheek. It was so refreshing and it gave me a feeling of strength and clarity. My bedroom door was closed and there were no windows open. Don't ask me how I knew but I just knew my mother was close by. I wiped away my tears and got ready for the funeral.

During the funeral I thought only of the laughter and the happy times I had shared with Mum. As her coffin disappeared behind the heavy curtains and I said my last goodbyes I felt a kiss on first my right cheek and then my left cheek. In my mind's eye I clearly saw Mum smiling and dancing, just the way she wanted me to remember her. From now on, every time I think of her I think of her always laughing and smiling.

For many much-needed reassurance and comfort comes from seeing white feathers that seem to appear from nowhere at significant moments. Here's Pat's charming story:

Words of a Feather

I was feeling really low. My best friend died and it was her birthday, a day we would usually have spent together with lots of drink and laughter. I started reading a book to take my mind off things and while I was reading in my head I heard her name. I looked up and when I looked down again there was this lovely white feather on the page. I put it down to one of those things but that evening when I was sitting by a window having a cup of tea and thinking about my friend again this white feather came floating through the window. Before it landed I patted it away and it fell outside but a moment later it was back floating in through the window, where it stayed in mid-air, just hovering. It was beautiful, and took my breath and my tears away.

For some people it is through dreams that angels bring their healing. Betty sent me this awesome letter.

Amazing Smile

I am at present enjoying your book 'An Angel Healed Me' and I thought I would share my story with you.

About twenty years ago I had this amazing dream and I can remember it vividly to this day because it helped me through a very difficult period in my life. My daughter had contracted a neurological illness which had put her in a wheelchair and she had just not long been released from hospital and was getting physio etc. She made a recovery but at the same time my mother had just been released from hospital after being operated on for lung cancer. So around that time I was looking after both of them. It was exhausting and draining.

I had this dream. I dreamt that I had walked into a church hall in the village where we used to live. The church hall then changed into what would appear to be a school gym with the ladders etc. round the walls. There was a group of people sitting in a circle on the floor. I joined this group but I did not know any of them.

Suddenly, the room started to turn clockwise and as it did so I started to slowly raise up, until I was sitting cross-legged almost reaching the ceiling. The other people were still sitting beneath me. I sensed someone to the left-hand side of me. I looked and there was this young man of about twenty years of age. He was wearing a white open-necked shirt and white trousers. He was sitting crossed-legged and had bare feet. He had a tanned complexion. He had short brown hair and the most amazing smile I have ever seen in my life. He turned me round and we faced each other. Then he took hold of both my hands and held them. He was looking down at the time. He had long dark eye-lashes and I thought he would have dark brown eyes due to his colouring. He was very handsome.

After holding my hands for a while the man looked up, opened his eyes and gazed into mine. It was like an electric shock going through my body. His eyes were amazing and I will never forget them. They were sparking and they were amethyst. He continued to look into my eyes or should I say soul because that was how it felt and then slowly he lowered me back to the ground. At that point, I woke up.

I have never forgotten him or how he looked even after all this time. It was one special dream and it gave me energy, strength and hope when I needed it the most. My daughter recovered from her illness and I feel he was there at that time to help me cope.

Like Betty, I've found that reassurance and comfort from my guardian angel tends to come from dreams, and flashes of astonishing intuition, when I least expect them, but I've also found that sometimes my angels can appear in human form. One of the most powerful examples of this happened to me about eleven years ago now, when my son was nine months old and an angel came to my door.

An Angel at My Door

I was in the bathroom. I can't have been there for more than a minute or so when the doorbell rang. I went to the door and got the shock of my life when I saw this boy, he looked about ten years old, holding my baby son in his arms. I'd only left my baby on the living-room rug for a quick bathroom break. He was crawling a little but not yet walking, so I had thought it was safe to leave him. I'd forgotten all about leaving the front door open after the postman came.

The boy told me that when he walked past he saw my baby crawling on the porch, dangerously close to some steps which led to a stone path below. A wave of panic ran through me as I realized how close things had got to tragedy that morning. Instinct took over and I grabbed my son from the boy and held him close to me, smothering him with kisses. Then I looked up intending to thank the boy and give him some money or some sweets. I was so very grateful that he had been there but he had gone. With my son held safely in my arms I walked down the steps and looked up and down the street outside our house. I was sure that I would see him walking away either to the left or to the right as there were no bends or turns in the street he could head down but there was no trace of him. In just a few moments he had vanished.

I don't know if this boy was my guardian angel in human guise but he will always be an angel in my eyes. He saved my baby from falling down the steps. I've been told many times by others that he was probably just a kind and helpful boy doing a good deed, but why would he not linger afterwards for a thank you or a reward. How on earth did he disappear so quickly?

Anne Marie wrote to me to tell me that her daughter Cressy had a similar experience.

Ordinary Angel

This is what happened. My Cressy was about seventeen years old at the time (she's now thirty-one) and she was working as a model for teenage magazine fashion shoots. She had been sent to a job in an unfamiliar and not very nice part of London. Coming up from the Underground, she consulted her A to Z to find the road and observed that some men over the road had noticed her.

A woman came up to her and asked if she was lost. Cressy told her the road she was looking for, and the woman said she was going that way and would accompany her. Cressy said that she was very ordinary looking, except that she was wearing a really bright white, polo-necked jumper and jeans. When they arrived at the house Cressy and the woman went through the little gate and up the short path to the front door.

Cressy knocked on the door and then turned to thank the woman. She had gone and was nowhere to be seen, but there had not been time for her to get out of sight. The road was one of those long, very straight residential roads; each house having a little gate and a short path to the front door. Cressy said there was absolutely nowhere for someone to hide and if this woman had walked nor-

mally away she would still have been seen, so it was very odd indeed.

When Cressy came home, she obviously felt it was an unusual enough experience to tell me about it and I immediately recognized the woman as an angel. She may have looked ordinary, but that was only to 'fit in'. After all, if she had appeared as a shimmering ethereal being with wings, Cressy would probably have been frightened! I personally think it is interesting that Cressy noted her jumper was 'bright and white' – I have heard of other angel encounters where the angel person is wearing something white. Cressy is the most down-to-earth girl, and would not have fabricated such a story. I feel that Cressy was in danger from the men at the station and the angel appeared to see her safely to her destination.

You may have noticed that none of the people in the stories so far actually saw angels in their traditional form, yet they remain convinced that angels dipped into their lives and somehow made them stronger, happier and greater than they believed themselves to be. From my research and my own experience it seems that modern-day angel encounters are less about full-blown angel visions and more about mysterious strangers, spectacular coincidences, the touch, scent, kiss, whisper, laugh and other gentle or invisible signs that angels use to alert us to their presence. But even though bright lights, halos and wings don't appear in the stories, this doesn't make them any less remarkable.

This is not to say I don't get stories from people who have seen or spoken to angels. From time to time I receive stories like this breathtaking one sent to me by Grace:

Remember?

After my dad was diagnosed with the early stages of Alzheimer's there were days when he was completely normal but there were also days when he would leave his house and just wander for miles with no idea where he was going. I was concerned for his safety and so he moved in with me and my husband, Ben. This arrangement just about worked for eighteen months but then Dad started to behave really erratically. Night-times were the worst. He would drift around the house rearranging the furniture. He also became incontinent and started to shout at the children and call them names.

I staggered on for the next two years as best I could but by the time my dad was sixty-five I was getting desperate. My biggest concern was for the safety of my children, especially now that Dad was lighting matches for no reason. I asked for help from my doctor but the more I asked for help the more tests my dad was sent for and the more forms I had to fill in. I felt trapped.

My dad found it hard to even remember my name. He'd look at me as if I was a stranger or an enemy. One night when I was trying to get him to rest he started shouting and accusing me of kidnapping him. It took four hours to settle him and I fell into bed in the small hours of the morning, totally burned out. I was so tired that I couldn't sleep and I just lay there crying. Ever since I left school I'd been too busy working and earning money and raising a family. I had stopped thinking about or believing in any higher power but that night I begged for someone to help me and to help my dad.

All of a sudden I saw a ball of light flicker beside my bed. I rubbed my eyes to make sure I wasn't seeing things and crawled to the bottom of my bed to take a closer look. Then I saw an angel. It was fairly small; about the size of a football and it was just floating at the bottom of the bed. It had bright golden wings and a long gown that sparkled with light. It was the most beautiful thing I have ever seen and as I gazed in wonder the most amazing feeling of peace came over me.

The angel floated towards me and I felt all the tension leave my body, as a warmth coursed through me. The angel hovered in front of me for a few minutes and then it vanished. I knew then that everything was going to work out fine.

My husband was asleep the whole time. I know it wasn't a hallucination because from that night onwards it felt as if a weight had lifted off my shoulders. The next morning social services called and I was told that a home help would be visiting for a couple of hours every day to give me a break. It meant I could start to get my life back together again.

For the next three years Dad's condition got steadily worse and in the last six months of his life he didn't recognize me at all. Despite this I still felt that there was a strong connection between us and sometimes he would look at me as if he knew what I was thinking. I also felt his love for me. The day before he died he woke up and raised his arms towards me. When I came over he looked at me and said my name. I longed for him to say more but my name was enough. My dad had remembered me, at last. The next day he slipped into unconsciousness and passed away gently in his sleep.

Although my dad's illness weighed heavily on his family my guardian angel gave me the strength I needed to cope when I was at my lowest. She opened my eyes to the world of spirit and this made losing Dad so much easier to bear.

Ellen also believes she actually saw an angel. Here's her beautiful story:

Cloud Spotting

I miss my sister so much. She died on May 7, 1994.

Before I got married I lived with my sister for a number of years and we were very close. The toughest thing is that although I loved her so much I never got around to telling her. We used to argue a lot. I think that was because we were actually so alike. She was only nineteen when she died in a freak boating accident. I fell apart when she died but in time I did get on with my life. I've got my own family now but there is not a day that goes by when I don't think of my sister, talk to her in my mind and think about what she would have been like now and what she would have done with her life.

One afternoon, shortly after Easter weekend, I went to visit her grave. As I put my fingertips on the top of her grave, missing her and talking to her softly, I noticed that the sun was fairly low in the sky. I looked up and for a short time a cloud appeared as the outline of a complete angel with large feathery wings on each side of a tiny body, wearing a floating gown with little feet below the gown and hands reaching out towards me. It had curly ringlets in its cloud-like hair and its face was smiling. I knew instantly what I was seeing as I had read somewhere about angels appearing in the guise of clouds. Here at last was my guardian angel. It was the most comforting sight to me and for the first time since my sister's death I had a sense that she was trying to tell me she was with the angels and that she was happy and fulfilled in heaven.

Stories of people who actually see angels in their so-called traditional form are dramatic and compelling, but I do want to remind you again that they are much rarer than stories of subtler angel signs, such as miraculous coincidences or mysterious strangers who seem to appear out of nowhere, lend assistance to a person in need, and then simply vanish.

I believe that my life has been touched many times by angels, but I still haven't seen an angel in its traditional form. As I said in the Introduction, this used to upset me and make me think that the angels had abandoned me, or that there was something wrong with me, but over the years through insights, dreams, coincidences and other incredible angel signs my perspective has shifted entirely.

Why Now?

According to a Baylor University survey published in 2008, an astonishing half of Americans believed they had been protected from harm by angels, and this figure rises to 68 per cent according to a recent Pew survey. Are British attitudes much the same? I don't know whether a formal study in the UK would yield the same results, but informal Internet polls suggest that up to a staggering 79 per cent of us believe in angels. I use the word 'staggering' because aren't we supposed to live in an age where science and reason have triumphed over faith and mystery? Aren't British people supposed to be more cynical?

The statistics don't surprise me. I never cease to be amazed by the response to my books and angels seem to have caught the imagination of the general reader. To date the letters and emails I have received, and continue to receive each day, number in the thousands – and just take a look at the mountains of angel memorabilia, books, magazines and websites out there.

All this suggests to me that an increasing number of people today are being touched by angels and/or belief in angels. But are there any specific reasons for this renewal of interest? I think a combination of factors have contributed and I will do my best to outline what I believe to be some of the most significant.

You might think that science has disproved the existence of angels. Yet it is possible to argue that the march of modern science has increased the popularity, and strengthened the case for the existence of angels, rather than weakening it.

If you look at quantum theory, the theoretical basis for modern physics, you'll see that it attempts to explain the nature and behaviour of matter and energy on the atomic and sub-atomic level. In itself, it does not suggest that angels exist, but in recent years a number of scientists have come forward to suggest that quantum theory could provide a mechanism by which non-physical or spiritual beings, such as angels and spirits, could exert their influence on the physical universe. It seems the experts have come full circle and are telling us that science and spirituality are not as incompatible as many of us might think.

The first presentation of quantum theory was given in 1900 by physicist Max Planck to the German Physical Society. Planck made the assumption that energy exists in individual units rather than just as a constant electro-magnetic wave as had been formerly assumed. He called these individual units energy quanta and by so doing set in motion a completely new understanding of the laws of nature, by challenging the fundamental principle of cause preceding effect and by assigning as much significance to the observer as to his or her observations. Planck's theory gave reasons to suppose that the universe was more than just a complex arrangement of physical matter but rather that it consisted of dynamic packages of unpredictable energy. This opened up not just the possibility of the interconnectedness of all mind and matter, but also of the possibility that angels, spirits and other supernatural phenomena could exist by slightly shifting the probability distribution associated with individual quantum events. Put simply, from a rational perspective, supernatural beings can't exist, but from a quantum perspective they are simply things that humans have yet to understand well enough. So, science is saying that people who believe angels are real could be right after all.

Another factor that has undoubtedly contributed to the renewed interest in angels is the steady and gradual decline of organized religion. In our secular age increasing numbers of people are either disillusioned with religion or not religious at all. Most measures of religion, such as church attendance, and religious attitudes are trending downwards, with the decline particularly sharp since the 1960s.

Oxford biologist Richard Dawkins puts his anti-religion case forward in his best-seller *The God Delusion* (2008). However, even though Dawkins is successful in presenting religion as a man-made, divisive and oppressive force in human history, he is less convincing in arguing that the world would be better, happier and more peaceful without it. And this may go some way to explaining why belief in angels has not declined when interest in religion has. The decline of religion has left a void in our lives, and a spiritual hunger in our hearts. For many people belief in angels can fill that void.

There will always be a part of the human condition that needs reassurance that the spiritual is real, that there is a divine presence in our lives, and that goodness will prevail even if that presence is invisible and at times irrational. Talking about angels is an expression of this deep-felt spiritual hunger. But angels aren't just for people who have left religion behind. As mentioned previously they are for everyone, accessible to all and can fit into any religious or belief system. As such they have become a much-needed uniting force, which in a divided world is incredibly welcoming.

Another crucial element in the growing angel movement has to be the Internet – that spectacular tool of communication uniting people all over the world. It has opened new channels for artists, writers and publishers, via social networking sites, to talk openly to large numbers of people about their belief in angels, and they are accepting that invitation by flocking to the information superhighway in unprecedented numbers. Just type in 'angel stories' on your search engine and be amazed by the millions of hits you get. (At the time of writing an Internet search I did for 'angel' registered 292 million hits.) Yes, the electronic ether has certainly played its part and angels have adapted themselves perfectly to this medium. Thirty or so years ago, I'd never have been able to share with a wider audience the fabulous stories sent to me other than in book form. How times have changed!

This is pure conjecture on my part, but it seems to me that the angels themselves may have chosen this time to launch a new campaign. In a world of people seeking answers angels today have a role to play, not a new one, but a crucial one. They are reappearing and allowing the veil between the invisible and visible world to be raised so we can know them on their own terms. They are emerging from religious strongholds and breaking through into public consciousness and into the homes and hearts of people all over the word. For me, the re-emergence of angels is the true key to the mystery of 2012 – not the end of the world but the dawn of a new era when limiting concepts about angels are disappearing.

Indeed, I believe that the year 2012 is a central point in our spiritual awareness and my evidence for this asser-tion is based on the astonishing and ever-growing number of people having supernatural experiences. Forget for a moment the warming winds, melting ice, increasing hostilities and dwindling oil supplies. Though these too are signs of the times, they are not for me the signs of the 2012 gateway to a new era, as much as the amazing personal stories of lives touched by spiritual healing that I am reading and hearing every day.

I believe the re-emergence of angels has never been more critical. Sadly, time has not always brought wisdom and compassion and the modern world remains one of pain, injustice and suffering. There have been incredible advances but this hasn't stopped things going terribly wrong with humanity. Images of emaciated children, polluted landscapes and a world bombarded with violence and terror are screened in our homes every day. We urgently need to know that there is still love and hope within ourselves and others, and that the forces of goodness are strong enough to defeat the sorrow, injustice and pain we see around us.

Today, the angels are guiding us to a new beginning, a new dawn. They are making themselves known to us through the voices of ordinary people with extraordinary stories to tell, because we are crying out for them. And the more we listen to and believe in them the closer to earth they fly, bringing with them their pure, unselfish and healing love. Using the experiences of ordinary people as beacons of hope, angels are now emerging as messengers of love and healing by reminding us of the goodness we have forgotten within.

Cynics may scoff at sentimental stories of angels transforming people's lives for the better, but instinctively we know that angels represent all that is good and loving. In times past people had no problem believing in angels, because they knew they had to choose between them and demons. Today, with so much conflict going on in the world, and with so many of us battling our own inner demons, due to the wealth of choices modern life offers us, we all need to trust that when the time comes we will choose what is right and true. Before we say or do something we all need to ask ourselves if our guardian angel would approve.

In my mind, the time has never been so right for us to be reminded that whenever we feel confused, afraid or alone it is best to choose mercy and love, to be on the side of the angels.

Frequently Asked Questions

More and more people experience angels venturing into their lives. Many people ask me specific questions. What do angels look like? Are they real? Why do they help some people and not others? Do departed loved ones become angels? Why can't I see angels?

If anything isn't clear, or there are questions you want answered, remember you can always get in touch with me. Details of how to do this can be found at the back of this book.

What Are Angels?

Angels are messengers from the invisible world of spirit and serve only what is good, loving and pure. They can appear in countless different ways. A rare few of us can see them in their traditional form, but most of us meet them in our dreams, thoughts and feelings or sense their presence in gentle signs, like the appearance of a white feather or coin at significant times. For others angels can manifest themselves through the spirits of departed loved ones, or through other people consciously or unconsciously guided from a higher realm. And sometimes they can appear as mysterious strangers that come to help or guide and then disappear afterwards.

How Can I Know When I Have Seen an Angel?

As different as all angel experiences are, there is often a uniting theme. Whenever you ask someone how they can be so sure that they have seen, heard or sensed the presence of an angel that person will often say they know they have witnessed the divine, because they have discovered within themselves a deep inner certainty and feelings of peace and comfort they didn't have before. Heavenly encounters transform lives in both visible and invisible ways, and encountering an angel always makes a person feel uplifted and inspired.

Your angels will never make you feel doubt, anxiety or anger. Their glow of love is their calling card and you will naturally feel warm and comforted by their presence.

Are Angels Real?

I've pored over study after study on supernatural phenomena and interviewed countless people about their experiences. There is no longer any doubt in my mind that angels exist and the afterlife is real. I didn't come to this position lightly. My inability to see angels as I grew up often made me doubt their existence. This doubt increased when I went on to read for a degree in theology at Cambridge University and found myself approaching the subject in an increasingly academic and sceptical way. Then years later an astonishing breakthrough occurred and I finally began to see angels.

I've lost count of the number of times people have told me there is always a rational explanation for encounters with the world of spirit. One of the most popular of these is that angels live only in a person's imagination. At first I expended a lot of energy trying to prove to doubters that angels are real. I would stress how angelic encounters have been recorded and illustrated in almost every culture for thousands of years. I would point to the vast number of angel stories I had gathered from around the world as proof – after all, in a court of law a witness statement is taken as evidence – but it soon became clear I was wasting my energy. Angels are spiritual beings and their existence cannot be proved in a rational way to those who have closed their hearts and minds. It all comes down to belief and to those who believe, either because they have an affinity with the message of love angels bring or because their lives have been touched by angels in some way, no proof is needed.

For those of you who have problems believing in an invisible world of spirit, I'd like to ask you about love, kindness and goodness. These are all things you can't actually see, but everyone knows they are real. Like love, you can't actually see it or measure it under scientific conditions but you can see the transformative impact it has on people's lives. It's the same with angels.

Even the most sceptical of people know there are things in the universe that can't be explained. There is another level of reality, another dimension, a spiritual dimension. It might help here to think of radio waves. We know the waves are there, even though we can't see or feel them.

Like radio waves a spiritual dimension also exists and when we are able to tune in to it miracles can happen. Angels are messengers from that dimension.

Why Are They Here?

First of all, it is important to point out that angels are not a New Age fad. They have been with us since the beginning of recorded history, perhaps longer, and angels are not about to vanish. True, their popularity is on the increase and, as we discussed earlier, there are reasons why the twenty-first century is their time.

Angels are here because they want to help us answer the big question 'Do our lives have meaning and purpose?' Over the centuries, there is no doubt that we have advanced scientifically but emotionally and spiritually we haven't changed so very much. There is still a very real need for us to understand the meaning and purpose of our lives.

If science and technology have advanced us so greatly, why are so many of us still hungry and poor? Why do we still have wars? Why are we still depressed and restless? However far the material world has taken us, human beings have spiritual needs and that is why the angels are here, and will always be here. To address our spiritual needs and to bring light and inspiration into our lives.

New technology has not eliminated our inhumanity to each other. We really need a spiritual lift right now – a big one; something to wake us up and get us out of a frequently violent and unjust mentality in the world. We need our angels and our faith restored in the goodness around and within us, and to believe that miracles are possible – that people, like you and me, can hear angels calling our names.

Does Everyone Have a Guardian Angel?

I believe guardian angels are with us before our conception, when we are in soul form. They accompany us through birth and are with us in every thought, word and activity we experience in life and with us as we leave this life and become again a soul in heaven.

There's a lovely story in the Jewish Talmud which says that God sends an angel into the mother's womb and this angel teaches a baby all the wisdom that can be obtained. Just before the unborn baby comes out, the angel touches it between the upper lip and the nose and all that it has taught the baby is forgotten. Similarly, in other folk sayings, it is also said that an angel shushes the baby in the womb, to stop it from talking about heaven, or to make it forget everything because if the baby remembered too much it would never want to leave heaven and begin life on earth. The word 'philtrum' that describes the indentation above the lip is from the Greek word *philtron* from *philein*, which means 'to love, to kiss'. Very fitting, huh? And according to some vocal experts the philtrum allows humans to express a much wider range of lip motions, enhancing vocal and non-vocal communication. Again, very fitting, don't you agree?

Whether we choose to believe in and recognize the beautiful presence of our guardian angel is another matter. The guardian angel watches over us, looking over our shoulders at everything we do – and the more we listen to that angel, the more help we will receive. It's a two-way exchange; no angel likes to be ignored! This is what gives us the sense of unease when we do something we know we shouldn't! Get it right and our angel will breathe a heavenly sigh of relief.

This brings me to the very difficult question of criminals and guardian angels. Do murderers, rapists and other wrongdoers have guardian angels too? The answer is yes, but for some reason or another, these individuals have chosen to deny their existence and live with a sense of deep unease. The angels can't interfere with free will while a person is earthbound, but in the afterlife, where only goodness and love is welcome and there is no place for evil and cruelty, wrongdoers no longer have any choice in the matter. They will not be able to ignore their guardian angel, and will not be able to find peace until they have truly understood the acute suffering and pain they inflicted on their victims.

How Many Angels Do I Have?

Angels are all around us, not in ones, twos, threes or even hundreds but in millions, billions and trillions, to infinity and beyond.

You may have heard contradictory accounts of how many angels each person has. Some might say we all have a guardian angel, while others say we have three or four each or too many to number. While I believe we all have a guardian angel who watches over us, I also believe that we have many more because in the world of spirit having one angel or a billion angels means exactly the same thing. This concept of one and many meaning the same is a hard one for the human mind to understand. Let me try to explain.

The angels only individualize so that emphasis can be placed on one specific aspect of their loving nature. For example, when you need to learn something they can manifest as teaching spirits, and when you need to discover inner strength they can help you find courage with the help of a warrior spirit. It does not matter to our celestial guides that humans add names or give characteristics to their angels to tell them apart. They have no ego and do not need to individualize, but because they know it helps our understanding to name them they are happy for us to do so. Bear in mind, though, that as you advance spiritually the less likely it is that you will feel the need to separate one angel from another – your heavenly helpers will simply manifest as an inner knowing, an inner light, an inner joy.

What Do Angels Look Like?

Doubtless many of us would love to see angels in their traditional form as so often depicted in art and film but angels are spiritual rather than physical beings. I doubt if any human has ever seen what an angel really looks like in the world of spirit. They don't have material bodies and it will be the same for us when we pass over to the other side.

Angels are non-denominational, non-racial and non-cultural entities and will appear in any form, height, gender, colour, religion or ethnic background that makes sense to the viewer. So, as beautiful as images of blue-eyed, blond angels on Christmas cards are, for many this is not the image of an angel they will see. Each of us will see the angel that is most revelatory and acceptable to us.

After all that I have read, I am in no doubt that the way an angel will appear to one person will depend almost entirely on their personal history – their culture, their race, their religious beliefs, if they have any, and their level of spiritual awareness. That is why, although it is rare, a person with a more traditional religious background may see an angel with wings and white robes, and a person with more liberal views may see angels in animals or bright lights.

Angels are wholly adaptable. For one person, an angel might be a feeling of overwhelming peace following the death of a loved one. For someone else an angel might be the Good Samaritan who arrived on the scene of an accident at just the right time to save a person's life and then cannot be found afterwards. For others, angels may manifest as coincidences or dreams, through ordinary people who give help when it is needed, or through anyone or anything that gives them feelings of hope, comfort and inspiration when they need them most.

Do Angels Have a Distinctive Aroma?

A number of stories do mention a pleasant aroma filling the air before, during or after an angelic encounter. Often the person involved will be the only one who can smell the aroma, even when they are in a crowded room. Roses, lavender, lilies and other flowers are most often mentioned, but also common is the scent of vanilla or chocolate and the familiar scent of a departed loved one's perfume or cologne.

In answer to the question 'Is there a specific angel scent?', my answer would be 'no' because the angels will use the aroma that speaks most to the person concerned and will be completely unique. For example, if the smell of coffee or of freshly baked bread makes you feel warm and content, then the angels may well surround you with this aroma to give you a sense of comfort and protection.

Do Our Departed Loved Ones Become Angels?

Many people believe that their departed loved ones are looking down on them, watching and guiding them in much the same way as a guardian angel. I've had a number of letters in which people tell me how they sense the presence of someone who has passed over and believe this departed person has become their guardian angel.

The idea that humans become angels when they pass over doesn't really come from religious texts but rather from books, plays and films. Strictly speaking it is incorrect because an angel is a purely spiritual being that has never lived on earth as a human being. In other words, a human can't become an angel. Having said this, I do believe that the spirits of departed loved ones can be guided by angels and that celestial beings can act through and assume the appearance of a departed loved one. That's why, for me, the word 'angel' is often interchangeable with the word 'spirit'. (In Part Four we'll talk more about spirits of the departed and the best ways to connect with them for healing and comfort.)

Should I Be Worshipping, Praying or Communicating with Anyone But God?

First of all, angels do not seek to be worshipped, just noticed and listened to. They are the loving expressions of the divine reaching out to us. Therefore it could be said that talking to your angels is the same as talking to your concept of the divine. If, however, your faith fulfils you and you don't think you should be talking to anyone but God, your angels will not be offended. The last thing they would want to do is stop you praying to your concept of goodness and love.

Angels will adapt themselves to whatever belief system you have. They are for everyone and they do not favour one belief system over another. People of all religious backgrounds, along with those who don't believe in God, tell me they believe in or have seen angels. So, in my opinion, whatever your belief system your angels will work with you and do what is best for you. To believe that you have angels who watch over you and guide you is not to deny God, but to have faith in the awesome power of goodness and love, in whatever form they manifest themselves.

Before angels began to reveal themselves to me, I went through periods of not believing in God, but what I didn't realize at the time was that I did believe in something, I just didn't understand what that something was. Over the years I have found my faith again. Even though I am not religious I call myself spiritual, because at last I understand what I believe in – the invincible and immortal power of love and goodness revealed to me every day by angels all around and within me.

Can Human Beings Be Angels?

We often use the word angel to describe a person who has given unconditional help and love to others. Although the term angel refers to a benign being from the world of spirit, and not to a human being, the broadest definition of an angel is to be a messenger of love and goodness, and so in this sense a person can, either consciously or unconsciously, be guided by a higher realm. In short, I believe human beings can do the work of angels and angels can manifest their presence through people, and in this respect people can be human guardian angels.

Can You Tell Me About Dying?

I think everyone is frightened of dying because it is the great unknown. However, my years spent researching angels and the afterlife have taken the sting out of death. The fear I have is simply a fear of change, of entering a new phase of my existence. I'm not frightened of my life ending, because I know that it will not end. In fact, it may just be beginning.

Regretfully, society surrounds the event of death with secrecy and few of us are really prepared for it. We find it hard to talk about death, or even think about it but the reality of angels proves that death is not the end. It is just another phase in your existence and so much awaits you in the afterlife. If you think about it, you start dying the moment you are born and when you go to sleep at night your consciousness leaves your body and travels to the world of spirit. In the morning you may recall some of the dreams you had, but in a sense it doesn't really matter whether you remember or understand your dreams or not, it just shows that every day of your life you are dying and living again whether you realize it or not.

I hope reading this book will show you that physical death is not to be feared. It is just another natural process and in this life and the next it is hate, fear, anger and guilt that kill life rather than death itself. Death is despair of the heart and emptiness of the soul. Therefore, there is no death as such only darkness when there is no light. For in the light there is no death, only everlasting goodness and love.

Can Angels Appear in Our Dreams?

They most certainly can and we'll cover this topic in detail in Part Four.

Will My Guardian Angel Help Me Find My Soulmate?

I've received many letters from people who believe angels have brought them together with their life partners, but I do caution against the concept of finding one's soulmate if it becomes an excuse to move from one partner to another in the search for the perfect partner. A more thoughtful and careful approach is more likely to receive the blessings of the angels. Having said this, it does seem that when two people are meant to be together for the development of their souls the angels can intervene in remarkable ways to ensure that the relationship happens.

For proof that this is the case ask any couple with a long-standing, happy relationship how they met. More often than not a series of chance encounters, coincidences or accidents of time and place brought them together at just the right time. There are billions of people in the world and yet their paths and their hearts somehow met at just the right time in their lives. Isn't that an awesome thought?

Will My Guardian Angel Help Me Become Rich?

Many people have told me that in times of need coins or cash seem to appear out of nowhere, or come from the most unexpected sources, and they believe this to be the work of their guardian angels. I often used to hesitate to ask angels for practical help, especially money, feeling as if any material needs contaminated my spiritual needs. Well, increasingly over the years, I have learned that the angels do sometimes answer our prayers for practical help. Often their answers come in the form of coincidence stories about surprise gifts, including money, being given to someone in need at exactly the right time.

On more than one occasion I've found myself at the receiving end of a surprise gift when I really needed help. Once when I first went to live in London and money was particularly tight I found £900 in an envelope in the street. I handed the money in to the police station, but nobody claimed it and it became mine!

Although the angels may sometimes guide us to unexpected sources of money when times are hard, I don't want you to get the wrong idea. Your guardian angel is unlikely to give you the Lottery numbers because in the world of spirit money or wealth has no meaning. Angels aren't interested in money because they know that money does not equal happiness. The purpose of the angels is to offer love and healing. It is the richness of your soul that they are interested in, not your bank balance.

This wonderful story, reported in the press in early 2010 and paraphrased below, underlines the theme of money not equalling happiness far better than I can. I know you will be intrigued, and maybe even inspired by it.

Free, the Opposite of Heavy

In February 2010 Austrian millionaire Karl Rabeder decided to give away his £3-million fortune away after realizing his riches were making him unhappy. According to media reports, Mr Rabeder, forty-seven, a businessman from Telfs, put his luxury 3,455-square-foot villa with lake, sauna and spectacular Alpine views, valued at £1.4 million, up for sale.

Also for sale is his stone farmhouse in Provence with its 17 hectares overlooking the arrière-pays, on the market for a cool £613,000. Already sold is his collection of six gliders (£350,000), and a luxury Audi A8 (£44,000) and the interior furnishings and accessories business that made his fortune.

'My idea is to have nothing left. Absolutely nothing,' he told the Daily Telegraph. 'Money is counterproductive – it prevents happiness.' Instead, he will move out of his luxury Alpine retreat into a small wooden hut in the mountains or a simple bedsit in Innsbruck. His entire proceeds are going to charities he set up in Central and Latin America.

'For a long time I believed that more wealth and luxury automatically meant more happiness,' he said. 'But more and more I heard the words: "Stop what you are doing now – all this luxury and consumerism – and start your real life." I had the feeling I was working as a slave for things that I did not wish for or need.'

Mr Rabeder made his monumental decision while he was on holiday in Hawaii.

'It was the biggest shock in my life, when I realized how horrible, soulless and without feeling the five-star lifestyle is,' he said. 'In those three weeks, we spent all the money you could possibly spend. But in all that time, we had the feeling we hadn't met a single real person – that we were all just actors. The staff played the role of being friendly and the guests played the role of being important and nobody was real.'

Since selling his belongings, Mr Rabeder said he felt 'free, the opposite of heavy'.

How Can I Tell Good Angels from Bad Ones?

Some traditions say that we all have a good and a bad angel that remains with us throughout life. Others talk of fallen angels or dark angels. Personally, I don't believe in the concept of bad angels as an explanation for the existence of evil in ourselves and the world. In my opinion there is no place for evil in the world of spirit and evil exists in the world only because some of us choose to worship it.

While our guardian angels only reveal love and goodness to us we have also been given free will. We can choose our angels, or we can choose to ignore their light. Because of this we all need to work hard on our ability to judge the difference between what is good and what is bad in all things, including ourselves. This isn't always easy, but there is a way of knowing, of being sure that it is your guardian angel and not self-doubt, fear and other negative emotions talking to you.

How Can I Know If It's an Angel Speaking to Me?

The voices we hear in our minds can be confusing, but there are ways to tell the difference. When your angel tells you something you just quietly know it. You may have questions going around in your head but despite this your thoughts are focused and convincing. You know what you need to say or do. Sometimes your angel can be more forceful and direct, but this is only if your safety or the safety of someone else is at risk. The feeling is much different from the noisiness of fear that clatters around in your head. If the thoughts in your mind are full of self-doubt, anxiety and judgement they are the voices of fear. The words of your angel are gentler, kinder and non-judgemental.

If the voices in your head say 'you are a loser', 'you always quit', 'you haven't got what it takes', 'you're stupid', then this certainly isn't your guardian angel speaking. It's your fear. Your guardian angel would never say things to make you feel distressed. Your angel might tell you that something doesn't feel right, or that this isn't the right thing for you and it's time to move on and try a new approach to find what works better for you. There may be no words at all; just a gut feeling that it is time for a change.

Angelic guidance is always uplifting, loving and inspirational. The guidance is often repeated many times through your feelings and thoughts until you take the required action. If you aren't sure whether you are really seeing and hearing angels or making things up, be patient and wait a while. Give it time. You will find that divine messages keep on gently but assertively repeating themselves, whereas the chatter in your head fades.

And, finally, watch out for a very common block or barrier in which fear tries to convince you that you are not psychic or intuitive and not qualified to talk to angels. I believe angels are guiding my life and writing, but this isn't to say I don't ever have doubts and insecurities any more. Sure I do. Even today, I often wonder if I am doing the right thing, or if my angels are hearing me, but I take comfort from knowing that my fears and doubts are entirely normal. In fact, psychologists have a name for this fear and that is 'the impostor syndrome'. Research shows that everyone, even the most successful and clever of people, lack self-belief at times but this doesn't mean they are worthless. It just means that ego, which is entirely fear-based, is trying to distract them from remembering who they are, from reconnecting with their angelic birthright.

Why Don't the Angels Always Save Us?

This common question speaks directly to the great mysteries of this life and we may never know the real answer until we have crossed over to the world of spirit. Perhaps this answer is incomprehensible to the human mind. Perhaps when a person experiences injustice or violence or poor health it is all part of their soul's path or desires.

People die because they are not immortal and we will all have to face the angel of death one day. What is confusing, though, is when some individuals escape a tragedy or survive an illness and others perish. Why did the angels choose these people and not others? Why do some people die young and not others? Again I don't claim to know the answers, but I do favour the 'it's not your time' theory.

Why Do the Angels Allow Bad Things to Happen to Good People?

For some people the law of karma is a valid explanation. This is not the same as punishment for previous actions, more a kind of spiritual compensation. Sometimes the greatest lessons are learned through struggle. Our guardian angels may shed tears with us, but they know they must not intervene, to allow our soul's development.

As humans we live in linear time, whereas the angels live in spiritual time, so we may never fully understand the implications of our actions or why certain things happen until we also live in spirit time. All we can do is live in a manner we believe to be pleasing to our guardian angel, so that when the angel of death finally visits us, not only have we left the world a better place, we can take our guardian angel's hand and fly without fear and regret towards our new spiritual home, which some call heaven.

If Children Are Close to Their Angels Why Can't Their Angels Always Help Them?

I've attempted to answer this question above when we discussed why angels don't always help us and why suffering and injustice happen. There are no easy answers, especially when children are the victims, and we may never fully understand while we are in human form, but I hope this upsetting, but deeply moving, story sent to me by Sarah will help shed some light.

Touched By the Light

I'm a survivor of child abuse. I don't want to go into the details here but I stopped being a child at the age of six when my stepfather degraded me. I don't think I will ever be able to forgive him or my mother for standing by until the day I die. I do want to tell you about something that happened to me when I was eleven. I'll never forget it. My stepfather came into my room as usual but this time I didn't feel frightened. I felt this surge of strength and power in me. I felt like I wasn't alone. Someone was whispering in my ear and telling me to stand up. I felt like someone was lifting me out of bed and placing me gently beside it. For several moments I just stood there staring at him and he looked really frightened. Can you believe it? A grown man frightened of a small child like me? He never touched me again after that.

This all happened over forty years ago and I'll never forget it. I've met up with many other victims of child abuse over the years and some of them have had similar experiences to mine. One told me that after she was beaten senseless she felt herself separating from her body and drifting away in the arms of angels. I hope you'll share my story with your readers because I think it might be of some comfort. I still relive the pain and fear and because of the abuse I went through I'm probably the last person to believe in angels but as I get older I'm drawn more and more towards a strong belief in the loving power of angels.

Is There an Angel of Death?

The expression 'angel of death' is one that is familiar to us all. It often has sinister overtones but there's a strong suggestion by people who have had visions of the after-life, or near death experiences when they hovered between life and death, that 'angel of light' would be a far better description.

Many stories have been sent to me from those who have seen angels days or weeks before an impending death. Also stories from people who have witnessed the appearance of angels at the bedside of a dying loved one. There are hundreds and hundreds of such accounts, and it's clear from these that angels are close by and ready to help us into the other world when death approaches. It's also clear that at the time of death angels radiate love and reassurance through bright lights and their familiar form.

It's natural to fear death but stories from people who have witnessed the presence of celestial beings close to the bedside of a dying loved one can help to replace fear with comfort and hope.

Do Animals Have Angels?

Even those who believe in the world of spirit may be dismissive of animals having angels or angels working through animals. It is often said that animals don't have souls or spirits so they cannot survive death as humans may do, but animals are made of the same energy as humans and, in my mind, there is no reason why they may not survive in the same way, and have angels or do the work of angels in the same way that humans do.

Anyone who has ever bonded with an animal will be aware of the strong, sometimes psychic connection that can exist between human and animal. Psychic energy could very possibly be part of the same energy as spiritual energy and so animals could have as much connection to the world of spirit as humans. Perhaps more so, given their often superior sense of taste, smell, sight and hearing, and ability to sense what is unseen.

Love comes in every way imaginable and attaches itself to every part of creation, animals included. Sometimes the angels will work their unconditional love through animals and I have received many stories from animal lovers testifying to the joy animals bring to their lives. And wherever there is joy there are angels. Therefore, in my opinion, animals may not only return as spirits, they may also have angels, sense the presence of those angels and behave like angels themselves.

Does My Guardian Angel See Everything I Do?

Yes, your guardian angel does see and hear everything you do, and not just everything you do, but everything you think and feel as well. Don't be too shocked by this, as we all have things we are ashamed of and your guardian angel loves you unconditionally no matter what you get up to. Your angel knows that your soul is on a journey towards the light and sometimes this journey will take you into darkness. Think about it this way. If you didn't look into darkness, how would you know how to recognize the light? Life on this earth is all about choices and your guardian angel knows that spiritual awareness and wisdom can only come from making choices, even if those choices are bad ones and cause regret and pain along the way.

Remember, your guardian angel never leaves your side from birth through death no matter what bad choices and mistakes you make. They will always give us their love and guidance, but it is our free choice whether we listen to it or not.

Shouldn't I Take Control of My Own Life Instead of Relying on My Angels?

Some people do write to me and tell me that they feel they should be taking control of their own life instead of asking for angelic assistance. I write back and tell them that asking for the help of your angels is not about shirking responsibility, because the job of the angels is not to control your life and do everything for you. They are here to offer you love and guidance but you need to make the decision to respond to that love and guidance. Sometimes they will help clear the way for you with divine intervention but more often than not their role is to give you the courage and strength you need to help yourself.

How Do I Talk to My Angels?

There's a section on communicating with your angels in Part Three. Hopefully the advice you'll find there will give you the answers you need.

Why Can't I See or Hear Angels? Why Won't My Angels Help Me?

Your angels are always around you and sending you divine guidance all the time, but there are a number of reasons why you may think you are unable to see or hear them. One of the most common reasons is trying too hard to make things happen. As you may have read in the Introduction, trying too hard was my barrier and the reason why it took me until I was well into my thirties to see and hear angels. I really hope that reading this book will stop you making the same mistakes I did.

Trying too hard to hear and see angels simply causes pressure, tension and self-doubt. Although you may be sincere in your desire to see angels, thinking you can do it all by yourself gives your ego too much dominance and your ego is an instinctive enemy of angels. Instead of straining, what you need to do is relax and trust that your angels will reveal themselves to you when the time is right. Stop chasing angels and keep your mind and your heart open to the wonder around and within you instead.

Another possible reason why you might feel that your angels are not with you or helping you is that their guidance simply hasn't been noticed, or it has been noticed but ignored, because it seems too simple or unrelated to your question or prayer and you don't trust it. And sometimes you may not be able to see or hear your angels because certain negative lifestyle habits, such as drinking and smoking or certain lifestyle factors, such as untidiness and noise, are interfering with clear divine guidance.

There's plenty of advice in Part Three on how to notice, see and hear the angels in your life and how to recognize and accept their guidance. Before you read on, though, take a moment to savour this beautiful poem by an anonymous author. It might help you stay in a receptive state, instead of trying too hard to make something happen.

May angels rest beside your door.
May you hear their voices sing.
May you feel their loving care for you.
May you hear their peace bells ring.
May angels always care for you
And not let you trip and fall.
May they bear you up on angels' wings.

May they keep you standing tall.
May they whisper wisdom in your ear.
May they touch you when you need.
May they remove from you each trace of fear.
May they keep you from feeling greed.
May they fill you with their presence.
May they always stand besides you
And make you ever bold.
May they teach you what you need to know
About life here and hereafter.
May they fill you always with their love
And give you the gift of laughter.

Author Unknown

PART THREE

How to See Angels

Angels are all around us, all the time,
in the very air we breathe.

Eileen Elias Freeman

So if angels are real, and all around us, how do they affect our everyday lives? How can we rise above the mundane aspects of our life to actually see, hear and feel them? In this section of the book, we'll discuss all this and more.

There is much discussion today of divine intervention in the lives of ordinary people, miracle healings and rescues and heavenly guidance. These stories can give us inspiration because they remind us that the day-to-day routines and mundanity of our lives is not all there is. However, as fantastically uplifting as these stories are, it is important to remember that no one should be left out of the picture because they do not have an angel story or encounter to share. That's why in many ways this section is the true heart of this book because it shows how anyone can see angels. Indeed nothing gives the angels more joy. They want every human to seek them out and enter into communication with them.

So, in the pages that follow you will find a step-by-step guide to feeling, seeing and hearing the divine messages your angels are sending you all the time. There are also guidelines to help you know if what you are experiencing is truly an angel, or the product of an overactive imagination.

Tuning in

There are many different ways to make contact with your angels but most people do so through one or more of the four following ways:

Clairvoyance: this is the ability to see angels, or to see the information they are sending to you. They can appear in their traditional form or in the guise of colours, clouds or bright lights, or perhaps you see a film of them in your mind. They can also appear in your dreams.

Clairaudience: this is the ability to hear the voice of an angel inside your mind, or just outside your ears as if someone was standing close by you. You may also hear music or your name being called, or a ringing in your ear.

Clairsentience: this is the ability to sense your angels either through your feelings, or through touch and smell. When an angel touches you there may be a tingling sensation as if someone has placed a hand on you. You may also smell flowers or perfume that has no discernible source. People with clairsentience often receive information through their gut instincts or get butterflies in their stomach. They simply know that their angels are with them even though they don't know how. People who are clairsentient are often extremely sensitive to the moods of those around them.

Claircognizance: an idea or insight will suddenly pop into your head. You won't know how it got there, but you recognize that it is divinely inspired.

Understanding the way you are most likely to receive guidance from your angels is the first step towards establishing contact with them. Think about how you interact with other people; this will give you some clues. Are you a person who thinks in pictures, or are you a good listener? Or do you let your feelings guide you? Don't worry if it isn't clear to you which method you are drawn to, or if you are drawn to more than one way. Just read all the information in the pages that follow and as you do keep observing yourself and thinking about the way information comes most naturally to you. In time, things will naturally fall into place.

Don't try to force things as you read on. Just as the food you eat nourishes your body, and some foods are better than others, so your feelings are food for your connection with your angels. A diet of competitiveness, tension and frustration will not draw your angels close to you; one feeling food you need more than anything else is feelings of respect. Believe it or not, respect for life, nature and the amazing world we live in, combined with feelings of wonder and good intentions are the richest foods to stimulate your spiritual growth.

So, keep the idea of respect in your mind and your chances of encountering angels will increase significantly. If you have problems grasping this idea, it might help to think back to your childhood. Was there someone who inspired awe in you? If that doesn't help, think of something spectacular and awe-inspiring in nature, like a rainbow or a sunset or a waterfall. The more you can tap into these feelings of wonder, respect and awe the more you will be able to receive the messages your angels are sending you.

How to Sense or Feel Angels

Clairsentience – sensing the presence of angels and the spirits of departed loved ones through your feelings or through your senses of smell or touch or taste – is perhaps the most common way in which people connect to their angels.

Listening to your feelings, and more importantly trusting them, is a reliable way to connect with your angels. You may have already received divine guidance in this way. For example, you may have met someone and felt uplifted or nervous for no reason; you may have felt the atmosphere in a room when you walk in. These experiences are common ways to receive guidance from above, but many of us tend to discount them. How often have you had a gut feeling that something or someone didn't feel right but you ignored those feelings and regretted it later? One of the most interesting things about clairsentience is that it is a gift most often ignored, or not even noticed by those that have it.

Some of the most usual ways that clairsentience can manifest itself:

- The sensation that someone is standing behind you but when you turn around there is no one there.

- Feeling that someone you can't see has touched you, stroked your cheek, kissed you or embraced you.

- A tickling sensation on your body – for some people it feels as if the hairs on the back of their neck are standing on end.

- Noticing a slight pressure on your forehead.

- Feeling a cool breeze from no discernible source.

- Noticing certain scents, such as floral fragrances or other fragrances, again with no recognizable source.

- Feeling that someone is sitting or standing beside you; even seeing an indent where that person or animal may have sat.

- Experiencing sudden surges of happiness.

- Sensing the strong presence of a departed loved one around you or beside you.

I believe we all have this natural gift of divine connection, but few of us notice it because it can often be difficult to interpret. Think about it. Have you ever had a sudden or inexplicable change of heart and wondered 'Where did that come from! That's the last thing I thought I would do or agree to'? You could easily dismiss that as so-called common sense or intuition, but it's the work of your angels guiding you in the direction you need to go.

Have you ever felt completely wretched, feeling a situation is hopeless and impossible to change and then out of nowhere everything turns around? You are filled with hope and optimism. It's your angels at work again. Have you ever felt forgotten and alone and then a feeling of warmth surrounds you. That's the touch of your heavenly guide to let you know you are not alone.

I often have the sensation of someone standing right behind me watching me. Then when I turn around there is no one there. The sensation most typically occurs when I am alone and working on my computer in my office, but also in crowded rooms or when I am outside walking on the street. There is no specific trigger but it is more likely to happen if I'm feeling stressed about something. When I have a pressing deadline and overdo the writing the sensation gently reminds me that it is time to stop, take a break, refresh my eyes and smell the flowers.

I have never felt alarmed by these 'look behind you' sensations. In fact, the opposite is the case. I feel joyful because I know that my guardian angel is right beside me, watching over me. I'm aware, though, that others who have had this experience – and believe me it is far more common than you think – may think their imagination is running away with them or they are being nervous or even paranoid.

My advice if you experience the 'look behind you' sensation is to breathe deeply and stay calm. Of course, you should double check that you aren't being followed, spied on or in danger. I narrowly escaped a mugging one night when I experienced this sensation walking down a back street in London a few years back. I turned around and instantly realized the nature of the threat and ran away as fast as I could. However, once you have established that the coast is clear – as it usually is – especially when you know you are completely alone in a room or place, celebrate the closeness of your guardian angel. Thank your angel for watching over you so closely, reminding you of their comforting and constant presence. Use the sensation to open your heart and ask for heavenly guidance and inspiration.

Do You Have Clairsentient Potential?

If you answer yes to any of the questions below, the chances are you process information emotionally and have clairsentient potential:

- Are you compassionate and empathic towards others? In other words, is it easy for you to sympathize with others and understand how they feel; often without them having to explain what is going on in their lives first?

- Do the moods of others, especially those close to you, such as partners, friends and family, influence you greatly?

- Do you smell things, such as lavender or roses, for no reason?

- When you walk into a room can you sense an atmosphere?

- Do you get butterflies in your stomach, a tense feeling or a bad taste in your mouth when things don't feel right or for no reason at all?

- Do you sometimes feel tired for no reason?

- Do you hate crowds?

- Does the outside world sometimes overwhelm you so that you need to withdraw and be alone?

- Would you or those who know you well describe you as sensitive?

- Are you afraid of the dark?

- As discussed above, do you sometimes feel that someone is standing behind you but when you look around there is no one there?

If some of the above sounds familiar, but you aren't sure if an angel is calling out to you, remember true heavenly encounters will always feel loving and warm, not negative and nervous inside. Celestial guides will lift you upward in wonderful ways. You will feel a rush of joy or euphoria without understanding why.

Developing Your Clairsentient Potential

When you tune into your feelings your life will begin to feel more fulfilling and colourful than before and you will find it easier to understand yourself, empathize with others and experience divine compassion and love. Listed below are some ideas and simple, practical techniques you can use to push the boundaries, increase your clairsentience and develop 'clear feeling':

Increase your gut instinct. Gut feelings allow you to assess a situation, person or surroundings you are in very quickly. The term gut instinct isn't accidental. The area of your body between your heart and groin is particularly sensitive to emotion and is said to have its own intelligence – hence gut feelings. To learn more about your gut feelings imagine that the area below the centre of your ribcage has a mind of its own that vibrates. Imagine that every feeling you have exists because of this mind. Now think about what your feelings are telling you. Do you feel happy or sad, nervous or calm? Notice your feelings and let them ebb and flow at their own pace. Now imagine your solar plexus and stomach filling with light that looks like bright sunshine filled with softness and warmth, making you feel at ease within yourself. Let this feeling of warmth spread all over your body and sense the energy of this light touching you deeply to stimulate your gut awareness and strengthen your innate clairsentience.

Put yourself in someone else's shoes. Empathy is the ability to pick up on the vibes and feelings of other people. Do you ever experience overwhelming negative feelings which have no cause? Then you could be feeling someone else's feelings. Developing empathic feelings can open channels of heavenly communication. You can work at developing these feelings anywhere, anytime by going to a public spot and observing a person without them noticing you are doing so. Now imagine you are that person. What would you feel like? What would it be like to live their lives? If you don't feel comfortable people watching, choose a picture of someone you don't know much about in a local newspaper or magazine and ask yourself what it would be like to be this person. What do their eyes reveal about them? In time you will find it easier to read people more accurately and see behind the masks people wear.

Pay attention to what you feel and where. Clairsentience not only speaks to you through your emotions or gut feelings, but through physical sensations. The next time you shake someone's hand or walk into a room for the first time pay attention to both your emotional and your physical sensations. You may notice a part of your body glow with warmth or tingle, itch or ache. If it is the latter perhaps they are feeling under stress?

Tune into touch. This exercise awakens sensitivities in your hands so it is much easier to use your hands to feel the subtle energies around you. Start by rubbing your hands together for thirty seconds, and then extend your hands in front of you with the palms facing down and about two feet apart. Now move your hands towards each other with the palms now facing, bringing them as close as you can without letting them touch. Now draw your hands back slowly until they are about eight inches apart. Repeat this in and out movement two or three times and as you do pay attention to what you feel and sense. You may feel a tickling sensation or sense a warming up and cooling down between your hands. After you have done this a few times you may want to ask a friend to hand you unknown food items or objects while you close your eyes. Focus on the physical and emotional impressions that come to you and guess what each object is.

Light years ahead. If your diet is poor and you don't take a lot of exercise it is often so much harder to get in touch with your feelings. An unhealthy lifestyle will weigh you down instead of lifting you up and it is one of the most common road blocks to receiving guidance from above. Taking good care of yourself, by eating well and keeping active and getting enough quality sleep, can stop you feeling fatigued and lethargic and make it easier for you to tune into your feelings.

Buy yourself a bunch of pink roses. Pink flowers, such as roses, or luscious green plants not only look beautiful, their delicious fragrance can help open up your heart, so buy yourself a bunch and every now and again take a moment to stop and smell the flowers. Rose quartz crystals and emerald gemstones can also help increase your sensitivity so you may want to place one on your kitchen table or wear one around your neck.

For the Highly Sensitive

Following the recommendations above will increase your clairsentience and your empathetic response to the people and places around you. You may no longer be able to ignore things the way you used to, but you may also see and feel things you don't want to. As exciting as this can be, it is important that you are aware of the potential problems and risks associated with developing your clairsentience.

The more sensitive you become to the feelings of others there is always the risk that you confuse their feelings with your own. You may find yourself taking on the problems of others, or feeling overwhelmed by their negative emotions and this oversensitivity can lead to exhaustion, despondency, irritability and confusion without knowing why. This is especially the case if you work in the healing professions.

If you find it hard to disconnect from others, it might help to imagine a way to separate yourself from them. You could imagine a protective bubble around you that no one can enter. Whenever your environment becomes over-whelming or you don't know how to detach from a needy person step inside that imaginary bubble. Alternatively, you could imagine cutting an invisible cord between you and them when you feel you need to detach. This isn't being cold or distant because you are not the source of another person's happiness – their angels are – and you are not cutting the thread of love, because that can never be broken, only the thread of fear and neediness.

If you shower in the morning, imagine the water from the shower carrying away any negativity you have uninten-tionally absorbed from others down the plughole with it. If you prefer a bath you may add sea or rock salt to the water – about a cupful – dissolve it well. Salt has long been renowned for its cleansing properties.

Remember, your angels want you to help others and be there for them, but not if you hurt yourself in the process. So, if you find yourself feeling overwhelmed ask your angels to help you see everything with balance and insight again.

Opening Your Heart

This 'how to' section has advice on tuning in to your heart because it is in your heart that your angels so often first reveal themselves to you. It is in your heart that their message of love and hope will first become clear to you. An open heart is the first step towards receiving angelic guidance, the second step is an open mind . . .

How to Accept Thoughts from Heaven

Claircognizance is knowing something without understanding why or how you know it. It is an insight, a thought, an idea that seems to come from nowhere, a sudden knowledge that gives you absolute certainty beyond logic. It is divine communication or 'clear knowing' without being told. Whatever name you give it – intuition, claircognizance, sixth sense, higher mind, hunch or vibe – it is your guardian angel downloading information into your mind, as well as your heart.

Like clairsentience, claircognizance is very common, but despite this many people have never heard of it because they think of visions (clairvoyance) and voices (clairaudience) when they hear the word psychic. While it is true that some rare psychics do have visions and hear voices, it is far more common for psychics to receive information from the world of spirit through claircognizance and clairsentience – their thoughts and feelings. If you are expecting visions and voices it is very easy to miss divine guidance coming to you through these channels.

Clairsentience and claircognizance are, however, no less powerful for being subtle.

Listed below are some typical, but often unrecognized ways in which the angels can speak to you through your thoughts:

- An inspired idea comes out of nowhere.

- One of those wonderful 'ah ha' moments unexpectedly gives you the clarity you need.

- You have an inner knowing that something is a good or a bad idea or that someone is lying, despite evidence to the contrary.

- For no reason at all you just know what is going to happen in the future, and your premonition turns out to be correct.

- You lose or forget something and then, out of the blue, you remember where to find it or what you were trying to remember.

How to Develop Your Claircognizance

As discussed previously, claircognizance can manifest in understated ways that all too often go unnoticed. You could mistake it for imagination, day-dreaming or fantasy instead of the divine communication it is. Here are some steps to help you increase your claircognizance.

Recognize it. Just recognizing that claircognizance is a legitimate channel through which you can receive divine guidance and committing to developing it will start the process. Pay attention to the thoughts that enter your mind. Don't dismiss them as foolish or not relevant or something that may be obvious to others. In the great majority of cases what is obvious to you is not obvious to everyone else.

Record it. If your mobile has a record option, get into the habit of recording the random thoughts that come to you. If you don't want to use a mobile, a simple notepad will serve the same purpose. Keeping a record of your insights like this will give your thoughts a chance to express themselves instead of being stifled or dismissed. It will also, in time, give you an opportunity to assess how accurate they were. For example, did your feelings of unease about someone you were introduced to prove to be true?

Ask questions. Get a piece of paper and a pen and ask your guardian angel a question. Write whatever comes into your mind, however nonsensical. It does not matter if what you write down sounds crazy. No one is going to read it but you. Don't think about what you are writing, just write automatically.

Get fresh air. Divine guidance can come through a quiet mind more easily than a distracted one and I have found a good way to clear my mind is by going for a walk, preferably in the countryside, but if that isn't possible a walk around the block will do. I have found it is impossible for me to meditate. Instead of relaxing and quietening my mind, meditation either makes me feel tense because I can't master the techniques, or sleepy because closing my eyes is the cue for my body to fall asleep. Walking briskly on the other hand and getting fresh air not only calms my mind, it also helps sharpen my awareness so I can hear my thoughts and be more receptive to heavenly communication.

Is This Really My Angel Talking?

Now that we've looked at the way angels can communicate with us through both our feelings and thoughts, I feel it is important to pause a while to answer a question: If angels come to us through our thoughts and feelings, how can I tell whether these thoughts and feelings are from my angels or me?

I'd like to begin by sharing this story about a little girl called Anna sent to me by her mother, Sasha.

Night-night

About a week ago I was getting my four-year-old daugh-
ter, Anna, ready for bed. I read her a story and gave her
a cuddle and she seemed to settle down nicely. This was
something of a miracle in itself because for the last few
months she had really struggled to fall asleep and there
had been quite a few tears and tantrums. I was at break-
ing point. I really need my sleep and when Anna can't
sleep, I don't sleep.

Tonight, though, had a very different feel. Anna
seemed very chilled out and calm. We said our night-
nights and then just before she turned over with her arms
wrapped around her teddy she looked at the curtains
across the room, smiled and waved and said 'night-night'
to them. I asked her who she was saying goodnight to and
she said the princess in the curtains. I asked her again
and she said the princess in the curtains. There was no
one else in the room at the time. I didn't pay much atten-
tion and just tiptoed out, praying that she would not
scream for me as she had done recently. My prayers were
answered because when I got to the door and took one last
peek at her I could tell by her breathing that she was fast
asleep.

For the past six nights Anna has slept soundly and
peacefully, and so have I. She tells me that the princess in
the curtains watches over her when she sleeps. I don't

know what to think but what I do know is that Anna isn't scared of being left alone at night, any more.

Anna is in no doubt that she has a guardian angel who watches over her. We can all learn from Anna's story, or indeed other stories about children and angels.

All too often when I share stories sent to me about children, adults tell me that they can't be taken seriously because the child is imagining it, but who are we to pass judgement? Study after study has shown that children are more receptive to psychic experiences than adults. In 2009, a university lecturer hit the headlines when he criticized parents for being dismissive when their seven-year-old daughter told them that she saw an angel at her bedside every night, which she felt comforted by. And quite right too! Perhaps she had seen an angel. Children, if they are truthful and well, should be taken seriously. They simply delight in spiritual experiences, rarely questioning if what they are seeing is real or pretend.

Children are more likely to see angels because they have an ability to suspend disbelief. They don't need proof or evidence to believe in something. Sadly, as we get older and fear and doubt creep in we lose this ability. Our connection to our angels would deepen, however, if we could reclaim the open and unquestioning approach to life that is our birthright.

All too often our grown-up minds make us doubt and question what we feel, see, hear and think and the more we doubt and question the more difficult it can be to tell if it is our angels, or our insecurities or just wishful thinking. So what seemed simple and uncomplicated when we were young becomes a minefield of confusion when we grow up and we have no idea if it is our angels or our imagination doing the talking.

Perhaps you've trusted your feelings or your intuition in the past and it has been proved wrong. Perhaps you had a good feeling about someone and then they let you down, or thought you had a great idea but in time realized it wasn't such a good idea at all. Or perhaps something or someone felt so right but then turned out to be so wrong. We've all been there. Often it is difficult to know if it is your angels or your imagination, but over the years I have come to understand there are key differences between thoughts and feelings and claircognizant and clairsentient input.

I'm basing the following on my own experiences. In retrospect, I can see how I frequently ignored or misinterpreted my angels, and for me nowhere was this more true than in my choice of partner. If I'd listened to my angels I could have avoided so much pain and heartache because there were moments early on in each relationship that didn't eventually work out, or ended badly, when a clear, calm feeling inside me urged me to back out but I ignored it because I was scared of being alone. I told myself I couldn't afford to be choosy. I let my fear silence my angels.

I can recall vividly my first impression of my first serious boyfriend. The first time I was introduced to him my hands went icy cold for no reason and I got a twinge of pain in my chest. I looked at his face and it became angular and distorted. I rubbed my eyes and his face went back to normal. At the time, I dismissed all this as nerves but, looking back, I know that it was something very different. It was a divine warning, a warning I ignored to my peril. The relationship turned ugly when he became abusive, and lacking self-esteem I stayed with him for far too long.

It was only when I started to listen to the subtle messages my angels were sending me that my luck in love turned around and I finally met my soulmate . . . but I nearly messed that up too. On my first date with my future husband I was clumsy and talked too much. I often do that when I'm nervous and trying to make a good impression.

I left convinced that I would never see him again. The only feelings I had were ones that told me I had messed up big time. I convinced myself that he didn't like me. There was no way he would want a second date, so I deliberately avoided him for fear of rejection. Once again, I listened to my fear and, once again, it was trying to sabotage my chances of happiness and success.

Fortunately, I had a change of heart when by accident I bumped into him a few weeks later. This time, instead of apologizing, or talking at a hundred miles an hour, something inside me told me to stop trying so hard, just be still, and try listening more to what he had to say instead. We did have a second date and a third and many more and have been married for sixteen happy years and counting.

There's no doubt that the thoughts and feelings we have can be confusing, but I believe there are ways to know when you are receiving angelic input that should not be ignored. I'll list as many as I can think of below in the hope that it will help you.

Quiet certainty. When your angels are talking to you through your feelings or thoughts, you just quietly know or feel it. The feeling of rightness is very different from the noisiness and chatter of fear with its long-drawn-out and confusing explanations that clatter around in your head.

Communications from heaven have a calm clarity about them. The details may change, but the central idea or intention will always remain the same. Unlike the voices of fear there won't be twists and turns and confusing changes of direction.

Gentle and uplifting. Guidance from above is also a lot gentler than fear. If the thoughts in your mind or the feelings in your heart are full of self-doubt and anxiety they are the voices of fear. Angelic guidance is gentler and non-judgemental. If the voices in your head say you are 'a loser' and so on, or make you think of worst-case scenarios, then this isn't your guardian angel speaking. It's your fear. Your angel might tell you that something doesn't feel right, or that this isn't the right thing for you and it's time to move on and try a new approach. There may be no words at all, just a gut feeling that it is time for a change. Divine guidance will be encouraging, positive and empowering.

Warm and safe. Angelic experiences will make you feel safe and warm, like you are being given an invisible hug. The experience will feel natural and somehow familiar. Fear-based thoughts will, however, feel unnatural and forced and make you feel anxious and afraid. Instead of feeling comforted and watched over the experience will make you feel all alone in the world.

Bolt out of the blue. When it's just you doing the thinking your conscious mind will gradually take control and interpret things for you. However, input from your angels comes out of nowhere, requires no interpretation because you understand it instantly, and often has nothing to do with what you are thinking about. Divine guidance typically feels like a bolt out of the blue, while wrong guidance builds up an argument slowly and gradually in response to your fears.

Leap of faith. Another difference is that your thoughts and feelings are usually ego-based and designed to protect you from failure, disappointment or embarrassment. Angelic guidance transcends these fears and may sometimes require you to make a leap of faith, or try a different approach or put your own interests aside to help others. Your thoughts and feelings won't require this of you – their primary motivation is to keep you ego-based – whereas your guardian angel knows that the love and good intention within you is limitless.

Incentive. Heavenly guidance always has one motivation, which is to enrich your life or the lives of others spiritually. Often there will be no quick-fix solutions and your hard work will be required. Money and recognition may follow, but these will be added benefits and not the key motivation.

It is my hope that by noticing these key differences your belief in divine guidance through your thoughts and feelings will grow stronger and stronger. You will just 'know' when your angels are communicating with you, and will use all your skills and good intentions to create happiness and success for yourself and others. Believing in yourself and your angels will take time, but the stronger your belief the easier it will be for you to not only receive angelic guidance through divine thoughts and feelings, but also to actually hear and see your angels.

Hearing the Voices of Your Angels

We've come to the part of the book I was most apprehensive of writing, because my mission has been to show that angel experiences are perfectly normal. However, every time I talk to magazines or radio shows or give interviews about hearing the voices of angels I am aware that many people think this sounds a little crazy. I sincerely hope that the information below will make it clear, once and for all, that hearing angel voices has nothing to do with going crazy, and everything to do with divine inspiration.

We all talk to ourselves, but do you ever hear a voice in your head that you know is not your own? It is not the same as thought. It is a loud, clear voice that guides and inspires you to take action when you otherwise might not have. It is the voice of your guardian angel calling out your name. In the Introduction I mentioned how twelve years ago I heard the clear voice of an angel calling my name. I was at a busy junction deciding whether to turn left or right when this voice – it was the voice of my mother in spirit – urged me to 'take the right path' and head in the direction I had not intended when I started my journey. That angel-inspired change of direction saved my life, because if I had turned left I would almost certainly have been involved in an accident that claimed three lives. Yes, I've heard the voice of an angel and although I may behave a little crazy at times, as we all do, I'm not insane. I've got all my wits about me. And I have had many letters and emails from people who have experienced something similar warning them of danger. As far as I know none of these people are insane either. Like me, they are ordinary people going about their lives, when something extraordinary intervenes to change their lives for ever.

Hearing the voice of your guardian angel is called clairaudience or clear hearing. It is the ability to receive angelic guidance through sound. There is a lot of confusion surrounding this psychic sense, but hearing angels call out to you is far more common than you might think. Does any of the following sound familiar to you?

- You sometimes hear sounds or voices that you know are real, even if they aren't happening in the real world. For example, a baby crying or a bell ringing.

- You hear a ringing in your ear.

- You can't get the lyrics of a song out of your head.

- You hear gentle music in your mind.

- Hearing birdsong is a magical experience for you.

- You hear your name being called, but there is no discernible source.

- You switch on the radio or television or overhear a conversation at the moment that a discussion relevant to your situation is occurring.

- You hear the voice of a departed loved one in your dreams or in your mind.

- The doorbell or telephone rings but no one is there.

- When you long for an answer to a question or problem you have a voice in your head that tells you what you need to do, or if you have lost something where to find it.

Of the above, one of the most common experiences is that of a ringing sound in the ear. It is something many people hear occasionally and it happens once or twice a month for me. In the past I never thought twice about it, as it is painless and soon disappears, but now I view it in an entirely different light because I believe it to be a way for angels to download divine guidance. If you aren't sure what I mean it sounds a bit like a very high-pitched whistle. I don't mean tinnitus or the harsh, grinding noise you get from serious ear infections – if the sound becomes too loud and intrusive seek advice from your doctor – I mean a gentle high-pitched sound that lasts for a few moments and then fades away.

You don't need to understand the information recorded in the message consciously – you just need to be open to receiving it. The information will be stored in your unconscious where it will have an uplifting influence on your thoughts and your actions. The next time you hear it, instead of rubbing your ears why not relax and let your angels speak to you instead? If you aren't driving, operating machinery or on a hot date, stop what you are doing for a moment, and let the divine wisdom sink in.

Who's Doing the Talking?

Ringing in the ear, overhearing conversations or hearing lyrics on the radio is one thing, but what about a loud, clear voice that you hear inside your mind, or in rare cases outside of it. What's going on here?

Once again there are ways to know if your experience is angelic. First of all, if the voice you hear is loud and clear, but in a friendly not threatening way, it is the voice of your guardian angel talking to you. If, however, the voice you hear is unclear or abusive in any way it is the voice of fear and not your guardian angel. Divine voices will also be positive and loving and require an immediate response, whereas false voices will be unpleasant, uncaring and require you to delay or dither. And if the voice sounds exactly like that of a departed loved one – the same tone and turn of phrase – it is your guardian angel communicating with you through them. Sometimes the voice may sound exactly like your own voice.

Yet the voice you hear will not sound like you talking to yourself. Even if you recognize the voice to be your own, you will know that someone else is giving you input. You'll also hear the words 'we' and 'you', rather than the word 'I' and the message will be to help yourself and others, not to cause harm or hurt in any way.

How to Develop Your Clairaudience

If you are sensitive to sound, and the first thing you notice about people is their voice, then it is possible you are naturally clairaudient. You may already be hearing divine voices. However, if you don't think this comes naturally to you, and wish your angels would talk to you, there are some things you can do.

Listen with your inner ear. Find a quiet place, close your eyes and put all your concentration on the right, lower side of your head, and wait. Listen to and feel (see below) the sound around you. You may in time find you have a particular psychic ear – meaning that either your left or right inner ear is the one in which you hear psychic impressions.

Feeling sound. Start becoming more sensitive to the sounds around you. Notice the sounds that you often take for granted, such as birds singing or the rustle of newspapers. Listen to what you can hear right now, distinguishing between sounds produced by lifeless things, such as doors slamming, and sounds that are alive, such as dogs barking or humans laughing. Notice what feelings each living sound inspires in you. Hear your thoughts and feelings with your inner ears. Fill yourself inwardly with the feeling of that sound. Try to connect with living sounds. Let them speak to you through noise and sound.

Listen to the birds. Just after dawn or in the peace of early evening, walk or sit in your garden, or the park, and listen to the sweet symphony of birdsong as the day opens or closes. Listen to all the birds singing and then tune into individual notes and vibrations. There is a deep and powerful connection between angels and birds and the language of one reflects the language of the other. Listening with an open heart to birdsong is a truly lovely way to hear angels, and invite them into your life.

With practice your sensitivity to sound will increase. As it does be aware that sounds you were previously oblivious to, such as noisy chatter or mobile phones ringing, may start to grate and that your need to seek out peaceful locations increases. You may also notice that you feel the need to talk more quietly.

Trust me, in time you will begin to tell the difference between the voices that come from your angels and those that are merely your own thoughts. Listen carefully and remember your angels will always talk to you in a loving and gentle way; self-talk is a lot harsher and more critical.

Seeing Your Angels

I've been at pains so far to point out that people who see angels are rare, and they are far more likely to show their presence in gentler, more subtle ways, but this isn't to say that angel visions don't ever happen. Of course they do and in time they could happen to you.

I should point out that there are distinct differences between messages from your angels and hallucinations. Hallucinations tend to be accompanied by illness and by a loss of awareness of current surroundings, whereas psychic experiences are not associated with illness or known disorders, and there is not generally a loss of awareness of normal surroundings. In addition, hallucinations involve seeing living human beings, but psychic experiences tend to involve visions of spiritual beings, such as angels and departed loved ones.

Stories sent to me have convinced me there are sane and lucid people who can and do see angels. These people have told me there were feelings of spontaneity and naturalness about their visions and an absolute certainty that what they saw was from the other side. For many years I didn't think I was one of those people. Like many people I expected my visions to be outside myself, not internal inside my head. I also hadn't expected to see angels in my dreams or in clouds or in other common angel signs. I didn't really understand the nature of clairvoyance.

Clairvoyance means 'clear seeing'. Although there may well be some very rare individuals with the power to see the world of spirit with their physical eyes, most of us see it with our inner eyes. Information is received in the form of visual symbols, lights, colours, dreams or images from the past, present or future from the world of spirit. It is almost like having a movie screen inside your head with images scrolling across it. Have you ever seen images inside your head? Perhaps you saw yourself passing an exam before you heard that you had passed? Perhaps you saw your children before they were born? If you have seen images like this in your head, then you might already be receiving divine inspiration through clairvoyance.

Seeing with your inner eye is a powerful way for angels to reveal themselves, but don't think that it is the only way. One of the most wonderful things I have learned is that increasingly they are finding more and more ways to show themselves to us. We'll take a look at some of those ways in a moment, but first there's advice to help you develop your ability to think in pictures, and thus your clairvoyant ability to see angels with your eyes, both closed and open.

Opening Your Angel Eyes

Even though most of us won't be able to see angels flying around us, most of us have the ability to see angels clairvoyantly. The secret to unlocking this ability is to allow yourself to dream, visualize or think in pictures. To think in images, rather than in words, you may want to experiment with the following exercises:

Swept away. If you can find an illustrated book of fairy tales and spend time just looking at the magical pictures. Think back to when you were a child and your parents read you a fairy tale. While you may remember hearing the story, what you probably remember most are the pictures and the feelings they provoked. Whether it was the sun setting, the fire-breathing dragon, the princess's long hair or the knight's horse, the picture was real to you. You were absorbed by it. For a few moments you were swept away by the story, experiencing it deeply in your imagination. As you look at the picture now with adult eyes, you may begin to notice feelings inside yourself that feel both familiar and new at the same time. This is a sign that the pictures are working their magic, and that you are getting through to your psychic centre via your imagination.

From I to Y. While the above exercise helped to stimulate your imagination from the outside, this exercise will help stimulate it from the inside. Draw a large I and a large Y close to each other on a piece of paper. Look at both letters and then cover up the Y shape with your hand and look only at the I. In your mind's eye, let the I transform itself into a Y. See the line dividing and turning outwards. Try it again, only this time, try to see one arm growing faster than the other. Do it again and see one arm waiting for the other to complete before it moves. See in your mind's eye one of the arms moving and when it stops see the other moving.

Picture this. First of all you need to choose a picture you like. It can be a photo, a painting or a drawing. Try to pick something calm or uplifting rather than scary or troubling. Also make sure your picture isn't crowded with too many things. Then you need to find a place where no one else is around and where you are not going to be disturbed. Take the picture with you. Now sit in a comfortable position with the picture placed on the floor or on a chair a few feet away from you. Take several deep breaths to relax. Now tune out everything else that is on your mind and look at your picture for a few minutes. Try to memorize every detail in the picture. Look at where everything is placed. What colours are used in the picture? What image from the picture jumps out at you? Then when you're ready, close your eyes and try to remember everything in the picture. Describe the picture to yourself. Recall every detail, however small or insignificant. Try to see the picture in both words and images. See the picture in all its glorious detail in your mind's eye. Perhaps the picture is even better in your head than in real life.

Now you can open your eyes and take a second look at the picture. Look at everything in detail. What did you remember? What did you forget? How many different colours were there? You will be surprised how quickly you forget things. If you have forgotten a lot, try going back to the beginning and doing it again.

Then close your eyes and imagine that you are slowly melting into the picture. Stand in your imagined picture, look at everything and see it all in your head. Take a walk in your picture. Enjoy it. Don't be afraid to use your imagination during this exercise. Your imagination is what makes your experience so special. Don't be embarrassed to interact with your picture. No one is watching you, so be as open as you can be. As you walk around your picture, try to start a conversation with people, if there are people in the picture. Enjoy the mood of the picture – feel it in every part of your body. Then when you feel ready, slowly walk out of the picture and take some time coming back to reality.

Cloud watching. Remember lying back in the grass and looking up at the clouds? Clouds can take on many formations, and your angels can help you see images within them to guide and inspire you. Don't stare intently at the clouds – the kind of gaze you would have if you were day-dreaming – and for safety reasons never look directly at the sun. Stay relaxed, and as you look at the clouds watch the shapes that appear. What you see can be quite revealing. Trust your imagination and your angels to help you see what you need to see. Remember, you will only see what your guardian angel knows you can relate to. By developing this technique you have a psychic tool you can use at any time, as long as there are clouds.

All these simple visualization exercises will help to boost your clairvoyant ability. You might feel cynical at first, but give them a try and you could well surprise yourself with the results in a matter of days or weeks. You might start to see images, signs or symbols that inspire you in some way. If you keep practising you might even be able to project the image outward and see sparkles or flashes of lights or coloured mists indicating that angels are nearby or even visions of wings or spirit beings. In the end, though, it doesn't really matter too much if your clairvoyance is external or internal. The important thing is that you begin to see.

What If You Still Can't See Anything?

If you've worked through the visualization exercises and are disappointed by the quality of your mental images, then it is possible you are making the process of receiving angel messages harder than it should be. Watch out for the following:

Doubt. As soon as you begin to think about what you see and question it the image will fade. Remember, doubt and fear are instinctive enemies of the angels. Just because you see something inside your head, does not mean it is not real.

Expectation. The images your angels send you may be simple or complicated, but whatever images you receive they will be what your angels want you to see, and not what you think you ought to see. Prepare only for the unexpected. Remember, too, that your celestial helpers are not so much interested in specific events but in the bigger picture of your life, so you may not see what you expect to see.

Attitude. The best way to receive a clear image from your angels is to have a positive attitude and believe that something inspiring will appear. If you are worried or negative the angels can't get through to you.

Fear. If you think opening your mind to your angels will be frightening, you needn't. Everything about your angels is loving and positive. If you begin to see dead people they won't look terrifying like in the movies – there will be a joy and a glow of light about them. And if you're worried about demons or evil spirits disguising themselves to deceive you, don't be. Evil spirits simply can't recreate the radiance and beauty of heaven and if at any point you do think something evil is trying to enter your mind, just ask your angels to brush them aside and they will. Remember, you are always the one in control and if you practise clairvoyance with an attitude of love and for the purposes of healing and helping others you have absolutely nothing to fear.

Unqualified. You may feel that you are unqualified for spiritual work because you don't think you have ever seen angels. We all lack self-belief at times but this does not mean we can't see angels. It just means that our egos, which are entirely fear-based and not psychic, are trying to distract us from remembering who we are, from reconnecting with our angelic birthright. If you take just one thing away from this book I hope it will be the realization that you don't have to be a psychic to see angels – angels are for everyone.

Denial. You may find that your ability to visualize makes you look more carefully at all aspects of your life, especially those areas that aren't as fulfilling as they could be. This can feel uncomfortable if you have been living in denial, but instead of being demotivated use these feelings to inspire you to make positive changes.

Past returning to haunt you. Perhaps someone or something in your past said or did something to make you feel worried about psychic development. If you believe in reincarnation it might even have been something in a past life. In the Middle Ages thousands of people were persecuted for not adhering to the dictates of the Church. Could you have been one of them?

Straining. Trying to force things to happen means you are coming from a position of fear and, remember, whenever fear is present it is hard for heaven to break through.

Moving Forward

Don't panic if the psychic barriers mentioned above sound familiar to you. As long as we are human perfection is an impossible state and it is only through challenge and setbacks that true spiritual growth can occur. Spiritually advanced people aren't perfect in every way, they have blocks and flaws, but they are conscious of these flaws and try to ensure they don't hinder their divine potential. In other words, we all have issues and could all benefit from healing our psychic wounds.

Do your best to avoid negative situations and people. Your interactions with others should be positive and encouraging. If you feel drained and put down in someone's company, then you need to protect yourself from them. Some people manipulate others through fear and guilt. It is very important to maintain your boundaries in dealing with demanding people. Helping others is good, but not if it damages yourself.

If it's impossible for you to avoid negative situations try visualizing white or gold light around you in an egg shape coming out of your head and round underneath you to completely seal you inside the light. You could also wear protective crystals such as quartz, jasper, agate or turquoise or whatever works best for you.

If your anxieties reach back into your past, visualize a thread connecting you to the person or situation that is holding you back and visualize a huge, golden pair of scissors cutting that thread. You are free now. Alternatively, you could write down how you feel about this person or situation and then tear up the piece of paper and bin it.

It goes without saying that positive lifestyle choices will help you move forward spiritually. There's a powerful link between healthy diet, regular exercise and sleep and mood and motivation so do all you can to take care of yourself.

Start asking your angels to come to you. Every night when you are about to drift off to sleep ask them to come to you in your dreams. And when you wake in the morning ask them to reveal their love and goodness to you during your day. If you keep doing this and keep your eyes, heart and mind open you will start to see them.

And finally, get into the habit of telling yourself you are creative and a psychic. If you do this over and over again, even if it isn't true, sooner or later you will believe it so change the record and tell yourself that you are psychic. It will become a self-fulfilling prophecy. I promise you your ability to see angels will become clearer and clearer.

Other Ways Your Angels Can Show Themselves to You

In addition to appearing in our dreams (more on this in Part Four) there are other wonderful ways you can see angels. Here are some of the most common:

Orbs

Our heavenly companions like to adapt themselves to the era in which they manifest themselves. The twenty-first century is no exception, and one of the ways they have been revealing themselves is in photographs as orbs of white or coloured light.

The orbs phenomenon is being observed and photographed around the world and even in space. The scientific and spiritual communities have taken note and there are now over a million searches a day for the word 'orb' on the Google search engine. It's always a wonderful moment when a reader sends me an orb photograph. Orbs present themselves in a multitude of colours including white, yellow, orange, pink, red, green, blue, purple and in combination, like a rainbow. Most typically these orbs inexplicably appear on a photograph taken of babies and children, but also of adults who are spiritually minded.

Transparent orbs were first captured by film cameras when a flash was used. However, recently digital cameras have been recording the same strange spheres of light. It appears that the new, small digital cameras are good for photographing orbs, because the flash is closer to the lens. Light reflects back into the lens more directly. However, even though flash cameras are capturing orbs, they are not the cause of them. This is obvious because of the millions of flash photos that are completely normal.

When people send me pictures of orbs they ask if they should get them tested to make sure they are seeing angels. As far as testing is concerned I have done my own research. I have discussed orbs with professional photographers, and although some say the orbs are generally down to the quality of the camera, or dust specks out of focus when the light from the flash hits them, creating a large flare in the picture, or is down to infrared light reflecting off particles in front of the lens and creating the impression of an orb, most photographers admit that not everything can be explained away by faults in the camera. This is because many of the orb photographs, from all kinds of cameras, film and digital, don't match commonly recognized image reflection patterns of dust, pollen, moisture or camera lens light flares.

I didn't know much about orbs until people started to send them to me. Now, however, I am absolutely convinced they offer proof of angels lowering their spiritual frequency to express their being in orbs that radiate light and healing. Most of us can only see these orbs in photographs, but I have received many emails and letters from people who see orbs with their eyes. Apparently the experience is similar to the way all of us see a bolt of lightning.

In some photographs it is even possible to recognize faces appearing in the orbs. I find this truly incredible. I don't know if these faces are of angels or the faces of departed loved ones, but in my opinion the majority are best described as higher forms of spiritual beings, such as angels and archangels. Like us, spirit beings are all unique and individual and their energy status and roles vary.

If you do come across an orb in a photograph I'd be thrilled if you sent me a copy. You could, of course, also send it for analysis but in many ways it doesn't really matter what the end result of that analysis is. In my view, what matters are the feelings that seeing orbs inspire in you when you look at them.

If you still aren't sure what I'm talking about just type in the words 'angel orbs' on the Internet and you'll find many engrossing images. If you open your heart and mind to their presence, and allow yourself to feel the images they can be a reminder there is more to see in this world than your mind can comprehend.

Clouds

Another way for angels to reveal themselves is in cloud formations. You might look up and notice a cloud shaped like an angel or a feather or clouds that resemble wings or even faces.

From personal experience, I know that cloud formations are a hugely comforting way for your guardian angel to let you know you are being watched over. About ten years ago, when I was feeling particularly sad because my mother died and never got to see her grandchildren, I walked outside with tears in my eyes. I noticed that it was a cold but beautiful afternoon with the promise of a warmer evening ahead. The sun was shining brightly in the sky and as I looked up I closed my tearful eyes for a moment to escape the glare. When I opened my eyes again the sight was breathtaking. In the centre of an otherwise clear blue sky was a cloud in the shape of an angel. It was perfect in every detail especially the wings which seemed to spread right from the top of the angel's head to the bottom of its billowing gown. The angel's hands were folded as if in prayer. What made the cloud even more remarkable was that it was stationary and clear white when I would have expected it to be moving. It was also the only cloud shape I could see in the sky.

I'd often read about angels appearing in the guise of clouds, but this was the first time I had seen one for myself. I knew then that my mum wasn't far away and somewhere she could see her grandchildren. The cloud filled me with a deep sense of peace and comfort and remained clear for such a long time that it will be forever etched in my memory.

The Heart of Nature

Clouds are not the only place to see angels in the world around you. You may see angel shapes or formations in snow, mud, rocks, leaves, or even shadows. Another visual sign that your angels may use to remind you of their presence is in flowers that last for months longer than normal. Some people have told me that angel shapes have appeared in crystals, most especially clear quartz crystals. I've had a letter from a gentleman who saw the shape of an angel in his morning toast!

Even the most cynical people can't help feeling a sense of wonder when they see a rainbow – not only a beautiful angel calling card, but a sign of reassurance and guidance. Birds, butterflies and wild animals appearing at significant moments can also reveal the world of spirit to us, while pets (more about them in Part Five) can teach us valuable soul lessons about love and compassion.

Feathers

One of the most common, if not the most common angel sign, is finding a white feather in an unlikely place or when you need reassurance that your angel or the spirit of a departed loved one is close by. They can appear on the ground or floating in the air. You may also notice them on television or in pictures. When you find a white feather, carry it round with you to keep your connection to the world of spirit or spend a moment thanking your guardian angel for watching over you.

Coins and Numbers

If you find pennies, coins, or currency in general, in an unexpected place this is a sign from your angels that they are there for you. Observe the date on the coin as it may have a specific meaning for you.

If you see repeating numbers in your life on numberplates, clocks, house numbers, phones and so on then these numbers could also be a visual sign from your angels alerting you to their presence. Although the numbers 11 and 7 seem to have a strong association with the spirit world, it does-n't matter what the repeating numbers are, the important thing is that they will have personal significance for you.

Other Odd Signs

A stopped clock, lights switching on and off, objects moved or lost and found and other unusual visual experiences that make you stop and wonder for a moment what is going on, can all be messages from above reminding you that you are never alone.

Coincidences

Another common but little-known way for angels to reveal themselves to us is in the form of coincidences. For instance, you may get a feeling that you should take a different route to work and by doing so you bump into someone who offers you help in some way. You may pick up a book, open it at a random place and the words you read could offer invaluable insight into a problem you are mulling over. You think of someone and then the phone rings or you get a text from them or you find yourself in exactly the right place at the right time.

The dictionary defines coincidences as 'striking chance occurrences' but when they happen to you they feel like so much more than that and I don't think we should dismiss what Carl Jung called 'synchronistic phenomena' so easily. Coincidences can have a major impact on your life, in some cases they can save or transform it, and I believe they give witness to angelic guidance. A coincidence appears as mere chance if we close our mind, but if we stop trying to question everything and acknowledge that we are being guided from above our lives can change for ever.

In his 1993 best-seller *The Celestine Prophecy*, author James Redfield suggested that the first step towards spiritual evolution for the human race is to pay attention to the coincidences in our lives. Millions of people were inspired by the book and even though I didn't feel in tune with everything Redfield suggested I applaud him for encouraging people to focus deeply on the meaning of coincidences in their lives.

This right time, right place phenomenon has happened to me so many times I don't even call it a phenomenon any more, I call it life. When I look back on my life so far, I can see how things have organized themselves to bring me to where I am today. Coincidence has played a huge part in shaping my life and I trust that it will continue to do so. Think about the people who are close to you right now. What amazing coincidences have brought you all together?

Consider all the situations in your life when things just seemed to fall together perfectly? What other coincidences are out there waiting for you to find them?

It is my firm belief that angels can sometimes show themselves to us through remarkable coincidences. And the more you notice coincidences and express gratitude for them the more likely you are to encounter them. Remember, feelings of gratitude have an astonishing power in the world of spirit and invite angels into your life.

Spirit Signs

Who hasn't picked up a white feather? Or felt puzzled when a clock stopped or intrigued when a lost object suddenly turned up? Who hasn't caught their breath at the sight of a rainbow or felt a deep sense of peace when, against all odds, things somehow worked out for the best?

I hope you will now begin to see that, even if you can't always see them with your physical eyes, angel signs or calling cards are all around you. You just need to open your eyes and your heart. Sometimes your heavenly guides will reveal themselves to you in direct ways but they are more likely to manifest in subtler signs and coincidences like those mentioned above. You'll know the signs are sent from above because they will feel meaningful to you, be gently repetitive, and often timed to coincide with questions you have asked your angels.

Noticing, or looking out for signs, shows your angels that you are open and receptive to their loving guidance. Remember, looking out isn't the same as searching. You need to be in a relaxed state of mind because tension blocks communication with your angels. If you're still feeling sceptical as you read this because you don't think you have experienced any angel calling cards then I suggest that for the next week you suspend disbelief and tell yourself that your angels are revealing themselves to you in various ways. Ask them to help you recognize their presence and make it your job to sit back and notice their signs and messages. Trust me. You'll be surprised at the results. Whether it is feathers, clouds, rainbows, pennies, wonderful coincidences or the well-meaning actions of others, I've seen incredible life transformations occur when people start to notice the small and big miracles that occur in their everyday lives.

Calling Your Angels

If you still think that angel encounters only happen to other people, I want to reassure you that this is certainly not the case. I can't make you believe in angels but I can show you ways to notice them. Your angels want you to notice them, but this cannot happen until you open your heart and mind to them. So, starting right now, try to think of your angels as close friends. Ask for their help and guidance. Invite them into your life, be open to the idea that they are around you and begin noticing them. Believe that they can help you in all areas of your life. They won't make decisions for you, but they can offer you guidance to sort things out for yourself.

Inviting angels into your life is the easiest and most natural of things. It should not feel complicated or difficult in any way. It should feel as natural as smiling or laughing. Below you'll find some more everyday suggestions to help you get in touch with your angels but don't get bogged down too much with exercises and techniques. All you need to do is accept that your angels are always with you, ask for their help, or some kind of proof that they are close and then keep your mind and heart open to messages. It could come through the words of a friend, through a song you hear on the radio, through a feeling of comfort or, most special of all, a calm, clear certainty that you are not alone.

First and Last Thing

Every morning when you get up and every night just before you go to sleep get into the habit of spending just a few moments thinking about your guardian angel and asking for their help. Today, our lives have never seemed busier but it can be hard to connect with your angels when you are rushing from one thing to another. Just a few moments of peace are all you need. Peace and quiet, remember, is the language that angels speak. You can find this silence by going to a place where you won't be disturbed.

I'm not going to use words like guided visualization or meditation here because I think when specific techniques or rituals are mentioned it starts to complicate something that should be simple. That's why, despite repeated requests, I don't hold angel seminars and workshops. I'm happy to give talks, answer questions to the best of my ability, and open up discussions with my readers, but I would never set myself up as an angel expert with recommended techniques, rituals or workshops. I feel that such claims, in particular those that require a fee, run counter to everything the angels stand for. Angels are not physical beings and they cannot be summoned by techniques or aromas, lighted candles, perfumed oils and so on. All these can help you enter a relaxed state of mind to encourage your receptivity, but angels cannot be summoned by any physical means.

I'm sure there are sincere mentors out there, but my advice is to follow your own heart when it comes to connecting with your angels. You don't need rituals or scented candles, and you don't need to know a specific angel's name, you just require an open heart and an open mind. Rest assured, as soon as you invite them into your life, they will find ways to reveal themselves to you, ways that are completely unique to you.

Finding your inner silence or the real you, the spiritual you, is the only 'technique' I endorse because it is something you can do anytime, anywhere. One way is to start focusing on your daily routines, and every precious moment of the day, with love and joy. Another is to choose one of the angel quotations listed in Part Six of this book and to spend time mulling over the meaning. Deep breathing from your stomach instead of your chest, especially when you are outdoors, can increase feelings of peace and clarity. You could also think about the people you love and everything in life you have to be grateful for, but often take for granted.

Finding a place where you won't be disturbed and listening to soothing music for ten or so minutes a day can help you to enter the 'silence', as can reading inspirational books, relaxing in a warm bath, drinking a comforting cup of hot chocolate, writing in a journal, dancing, painting, drawing, singing, drumming, gardening, walking along the seashore, cloud watching or listening to birdsong.

There are so many different ways to still your mind and focus on the stillness inside. Anything you love doing that takes you to a place of peace, calm and joy makes a clearer channel for your angels to reach you; use those moments of quiet reflection to ask your angels for guidance.

I believe that sincere intention, feelings of gratitude and awe and an earnest desire to see them are always the best ways to establish contact with your angels. Don't let your fear tell you that you are not worthy of their help. Your angels love you unconditionally, and will offer you guidance on both monumental and trivial requests, whether those requests are to protect you or those you care about, or help you find a soulmate, fantastic friends, a wonderful job, a great house, a lost object, a parking space or anything else you need. Whatever you have to say they always have time for you.

Your Angels Want to Help You. All You Need to Do Is *Ask* Them

You can call your angels to your side by thinking about them and asking for their help. Get into the habit every day of finding ways to still your mind and inviting them into your life. If you don't ask, you rarely get and it's the same with your angels. Ask for their help and signs from them that you can easily notice, talk to them, share your dreams with them and then follow the divine guidance they give you. If you don't think you can see or hear them or don't understand the messages, keep repeating your question over and over again and keep asking for increased clarity. The more you practise, the more you will begin to recognize their divine guidance.

It All Starts with You

The more you talk to and listen to your angels, and see the goodness that resides within you and all around you, the more you will play your part in creating a peaceful and joyful world. It really does all start with you, and only you.

PART FOUR

Visions in the Night

*While we are sleeping, angels have
conversations with our souls.*

Author unknown

'Angels in the night' is the theme of this chapter. Not 'night' in the sense of evil and darkness, but 'night' in the sense of angels entering our dreams while we are asleep, or when we lose consciousness, and appearing in the guise of loved ones who have crossed over from this world to the next.

Not only can angels and the spirits of departed loved ones show themselves in our dreams, they can provide important guidance while we are in the dream state. For me, it was through dreams that I first made contact with the world of spirit. It was the breakthrough I had been waiting for all my life. I think the angels often choose this medium to first reveal themselves because it is one of the gentlest ways. While we are sleeping they can enter our unconscious mind, the place where real magic and transformation begins.

Dream Working

Have you ever woken up feeling absolutely exhausted for no apparent reason?

We have probably all felt this at some time or another. Perhaps you went to bed at a reasonable time, didn't eat late or do anything strenuous the day before, and had nine or so hours of uninterrupted sleep but when you woke up you still felt drained. Of course, there could be medical or emotional reasons for this, and you should eliminate these possibilities, but if you or your doctor can't find any logical reason I'd like you to consider the possibility that in spirit you have had a very busy night indeed.

Mull over this: dreams – and we all have them, even if we can't remember them – prove that when we go to sleep our consciousness continues to experience and explore while our physical bodies are asleep. It's entirely possible then that our consciousness can leave our physical bodies and be drawn to spiritual or healing work. Perhaps you were the spiritual presence that helped someone pass over to the other side or perhaps your non-physical body offered comfort or healing to those who are feeling vulnerable in some way. You may be one of those rare people who remember undertaking a spiritual assignment in your sleep, but most likely you are among the majority who don't have any recollection, just a vague feeling when you wake up that something incredible has happened.

Isn't it an awesome thought that when we go to sleep we all have the potential to become angels and be there for others in times of need? I'd like you to hold this thought, because it will open your mind to the possibility that dreams can be very significant spiritual experiences. Most of us lead busy lives and barely think about our dreams but when we dream the barriers of disbelief and fear are lifted and we have greater access to the world of spirit than when we are awake. That's why as angelic calling cards dreams fall into a class of their own, and why I urge you to pay much greater attention to your night-time adventures.

In Your Dreams

One night I dreamed I was a butterfly, fluttering hither and thither, content with my lot. Suddenly I awoke and I was Chuang-txu again. Who am I in reality? A butterfly dreaming of Chuang-txu or Chuang-txu imagining that he was a butterfly?

Chuang-txu (3rd century BC)

Dreams are mysterious and elusive. Some are quickly forgotten the minute you wake up but others can linger for a lifetime. They can make you feel happy, sad, scared, confused, angry or triumphant. In your dreams you can do things you would never be able to do in your waking life. You enter a realm where the extraordinary is commonplace and sometimes everything feels so real – as if the sensations and images you are experiencing are actually happening – but then you wake up and can't make sense of what you have seen.

I've studied dreams for decades now – and written my fair share of dream dictionaries – and I'm in no doubt that dreams affect our lives far more than we realize and can provide extraordinary insights into the inner working of our minds.

However much they may confound us, dreams have the power to heal and enlighten us and increasingly psychologists are regarding dreams as a mood-regulating system that can help people work through their problems. I believe angels can choose dreams as a way to communicate with you to offer their guidance and insight.

Everybody, regardless of age and background, dreams several times every night and some estimates suggest we may have over 100,000 dreams in the course of our lives. That's a whole lot of dreaming. Many people think they don't dream because they can't remember their dreams and have got into the habit of forgetting them. Just as our memories of heaven begin to fade from the moment we are born, dreams fade almost instantly from memory on waking.

Recalling Your Dreams

If you can't recall your dreams it's much harder for you to consciously receive teachings from your angels, so the first step is to get into the habit of remembering your dreams. It's much easier than you think. The more attention you give to dreams the more likely you are to recall yours when you wake up. Just reading this section of the book before you fall asleep may well trigger a dream memory the next morning.

The two easiest methods to ensure you recall a dream are to programme your mind for dream recall and to keep a dream diary.

To begin programming yourself to remember dreams you need to talk to yourself in a positive way. Just before you drift off to sleep tell yourself that you will remember what you have dreamed when you wake up. Don't tell yourself not to forget your dream, because your mind works better with positives and will focus on the 'not' rather than the 'remember'. Simply tell yourself that you will remember your dreams.

The next step is to keep a pen and paper beside your bed and keep a record of your dreams. There have probably been times when you have woken up in the morning and felt sure you have had an amazing dream but you couldn't fully recall it. This has happened to me many times. I've woken up with images and insights in my head, but by the time I'm dressed and ready to start the day the dream has vanished. If, however, I immediately write down my dream as soon as I wake up, I create a reminder to help me remember and work out what my dream is trying to tell me.

Keeping a Dream Diary

Even if you feel sceptical about the idea of angels entering your dream space, do try writing down your dreams, because the exercise will be incredibly rewarding.

Keep a notebook and pen beside your bed so that you can record a dream instantly. Even if it is in the early hours of the morning don't leave it until your alarm clock goes off, record your dreams straight away. If you don't do it immediately you will probably forget everything and lose a valuable dream.

There are different ways to keep a dream diary. Many people find that if they write the day and date of the following day down before they go to sleep this acts as a kind of trigger. Should you wake up in the night try to write down what you can even if you feel very tired and groggy. Then in the morning when you wake up you can add more details. Some people find it easier to keep a simple tape recorder beside their bed so they can speak into it when they wake up and then later in the day record their impressions in the diary.

Think about every aspect of your dream when you write it down or record it, even if it doesn't seem to make any sense at the time. Who were the people in your dream? Are they people you know or are they strangers, animals or magical creatures? Did you appear in your dream or did it seem like you were watching everything? Where did all the action take place? How did you feel? Did you have any sense of time or date or the season? Record the colours, numbers or shapes, the prominent symbols or stories and how the dream began and ended. Did anything in your dream strike you as particularly significant?

Now divide your dream into elements and look at each of them personally. What do they mean to you? Then look at the general theme or overview of your dream and see how it could apply to situations in your waking life? Is a solution or perspective being offered or is your dream revealing your true or hidden feelings about someone or something?

If you did not remember any of your dreams when you woke up, write down in your journal how you felt when you woke up. This will help you get into the habit of keeping your dream journal and will encourage your dreaming mind to supply you with helpful information.

I've been keeping a regular dream journal for close to three decades now and the more I thought about my dreams and wrote them down the more I started to remember them. It wasn't long before a notebook was replaced by a folder and then a file. In time my dream files grew so overwhelming that I had to record my dreams on my laptop. It's fascinating to look back on my dreams over the decades. In the great majority of cases they offer incredible insights into my spiritual and psychic growth. You see, a single dream is often only one tiny piece of a gigantic puzzle and substantially better results are achieved when I analyse a series of my dreams over weeks, months, even years.

However surreal or trivial they appear I know that every dream I have has some message or insight from my angels to offer me. It would be a shame to miss them, and that's why I strongly recommend keeping a dream journal. Nothing fancy is required – just a paper and a pen beside your bed and the dedication to use them.

Decoding Your Dreams

Once you've got into the habit of recording your dreams you need to learn how to interpret them. According to the

Talmud, 'A dream which is not interpreted is like a letter which is not read.' The problem here is that dream messages aren't always straightforward, and the reason is that in our dreams the angels speak to us in a different language – the language of symbols. The symbols in your dreams are all your thoughts and feelings turned into a series of images or word pictures. These word pictures are typically ones that your dreaming mind has selected from things in your waking life, triggering memories, associations or issues that link in with your present or past circumstances. They are often dismissed as nonsense when in fact they can be very profound.

Although the images and symbols in your dreams are like codes that need to be cracked their aim is not to confuse you in any way. Your dreaming mind is simply trying to speak to you in the only way it can and if you ever find that you get angry, tearful or frustrated when working with your dreams move on to something else for a while until you feel ready to return. Dream interpretation simply won't work if you feel anxious or are approaching it with a closed mind. The best results for dream interpretation, as with most things in life, are achieved with an open mind and a calm focus.

Whenever people write to me to ask the meaning of their dream I always urge them to think about what their dream symbols mean to them *personally* before consulting dream books. There are books on the market to help you interpret your dream images but although these books are useful, I think the best book to help you understand your dreams is your own dream journal. This is because the more attention you pay to your dreams the more you will recognize what your personal dream images or symbols are and what they mean to you. Each dream symbol is unique to the dreamer. For instance, if you are a horse lover, the appearance of a horse in a dream will be positive and uplifting, and it will have a completely different meaning from someone who feels nervous around horses.

Also don't feel that you need to interpret every single dream you have. Some dreams are extremely vivid and powerful and clearly rich in meaning, but other dreams can be less compelling, trivial even, or in the case of dreams where you find yourself on a sandy beach relaxing in the sunshine while the waves lap on the shore, just to be enjoyed. You don't always need to interpret everything your dreaming mind passes on to you. Work with what you can and let the rest go.

In fact, trying to interpret dreams literally can be harmful. It's a common mistake to make and a lot of people worry that their dreams may be prophetic, but this is rarely the case. Your dreaming mind is simply using certain symbols to convey important messages to you. Take dreams about the death of a loved one, for instance. This doesn't actually mean that the life of a loved one is in danger. It simply means that the relationship between you and your loved one is undergoing a period of change, or that it needs to change in some way if it is to survive and flourish. For example, if your child is leaving home and you have a dream about that child dying, the dream is a clear message that even though your child is growing up and leaving their childhood behind this doesn't mean you need to grow apart from each other. More that the relationship dynamics between you are changing and growing.

Night School

The advice to 'sleep on it' is age old and sound because when we go to sleep we give ourselves the opportunity to consider issues in our waking lives from a different perspective – that of our unconscious. Even if we don't remember our dreams, most of us feel better when we wake up the next morning. We feel better because while we were sleeping angels have spoken to us on an unconscious level, and this can help change our attitude.

Bear in mind that the great majority of dreams you have are symbolic and should not be taken literally and you will need to do some self-analysis to get to the real message. I regard these dreams as wonderful gifts from the angels because they offer tools for greater self-awareness and spiritual transformation. They highlight feelings, hopes and fears so that issues in your waking life can be resolved and hidden strengths and creativity revealed. However, a very small percentage of dreams have a very different feel about them. These dreams can't be compared with other dreams because they are so lucid and clear that taking them literally is the only option. I call such dreams night visions, and it is in these visions that angels or spirits of departed loved ones may actually reveal themselves to you.

Night Visions

If you don't know whether you have had a dream or a night vision, or visitation from an angel or spirit of a departed loved one, the distinguishing characteristic is that night visions are brilliantly vivid and impossible to forget. The dream will seem as real as your waking life and you will remember it in detail for days, weeks, months and years afterwards. You don't know how or why but you know that your night vision was more than just a dream.

I always feel that examples from real life speak louder than words so I've enclosed below an extract from a letter recently sent to me by Ella. I'm in no doubt, and Ella is in no doubt, that she experienced a night vision.

Heart Full of Love

My mother died suddenly from a heart attack two weeks before my baby son was born. I was an only child and my mum raised me alone. We didn't have any family but we had each other. We were incredibly close. We finished each other's sentences. I loved her more than I loved myself. There I was at the age of twenty-seven, alone just as my mother had been when she was pregnant with me. With no one to talk to and a baby to plan for, I didn't have the time or the opportunity to grieve properly. My heart was torn in two and somehow I had to find room in it for a new love – my unborn child.

Because I had no support, the burden was mine alone. I organized the funeral but a part of me went into denial. I pretended she hadn't died. I couldn't cope with her loss. A week before my baby was due I became even more depressed. I didn't think I could bond with my baby when it was born. Lonely and heartbroken I was convinced I was going to die just like Mum and it would be better if my baby was taken into care.

Eleven days after Mum had died I woke up in the middle of the night with a sense of something lingering in my mind. I had been dreaming but I had the sense that it was more than a dream. Mum had not been there but someone had spoken to me, telling me something important. I tried to remember it but it was like trying to grasp at clouds. Then I suddenly remembered the entire dream in every detail.

In my dream an angel with huge purple wings and bright yellow light all around her – I think it was a her – told me that my mum wanted me to know that she was fine. I would be with her again but it was not my time to be with her now. I needed to stay in this world and take care of my son.

A son! I hadn't considered the possibility. I had been convinced I would have a girl just like Mum had me. That was just the way it was going to be because it was all I knew. I fell asleep again trying to dismiss the dream as a meaningless fantasy and wondering why if it truly was a message from Mum she hadn't appeared herself. Yet, a part of me recalled the feeling that I could absolutely trust the angel's words.

The next morning I woke up and this time I had another powerful image in my mind. I had dreamed again and Mum herself had appeared to me. She looked beautiful and very happy. She was aware of my depression and grief but told me that I shouldn't be sad because she was alive in my heart and in the heart of my unborn son. I told her I missed her so much. She smiled and said that *from now on if I needed to see her I could meet her in my dreams.*

All that day I couldn't get the dream out of my head. Was it real or just the fantasy of a grief-stricken and heavily pregnant woman?

Two days later my baby son, Leon, was born. I didn't think my heart could fill with love again but as soon as I held him it overflowed.

Leon is ten years old now and the light of my life. I still miss Mum deeply but dreams of her continue and reassure me that she and I are still connected. Mum kept her promise and she has transcended time and place to visit me.

Eyes Wide Shut

One gentle way for angels and deceased love ones to connect with us is through night visions, because when we're asleep our hearts and minds are more open and receptive to receiving messages from the world of spirit. Night visions are also perhaps the best way for spirits of loved ones to reassure us without causing alarm, especially to those with a nervous disposition. After my mother's death, like Ella I was also broken-hearted and longed to sense and feel her around me. The medium she eventually chose was my dreams. With the benefit of hindsight I can see that it was absolutely the best choice for me because I just wasn't ready for anything else. I was too full of self-doubt, tension and fear and this would have closed my eyes, heart and mind to anything else.

Remember, if you still aren't sure if you've had a dream or a night vision, or visitation from an angel or a departed loved one, a dream is something you remember immediately on waking, but then it fades from your memory if you don't record it immediately. A night vision on the other hand feels like a dream but you will recall it vividly, even if you don't write it down when you wake up. It will stay with you all day and sometimes for weeks and months afterwards . . . maybe even for ever. You just know that your experience was real because in your vision there was a heightened reality you could feel, touch and sense. And your inner knowing would be right because it is through such potent visions, and with your eyes wide shut, that angels are showing themselves to you.

Parting Visions

Perhaps no night vision is more compelling and gripping than a parting vision of the recently departed. This is without question the kind of dream I get the most correspondence about and which I am most often asked about. In the great majority of cases the people who have these dreams are absolutely convinced that they were actually visited by the spirit of a loved one and that they received a message of comfort.

Psychologists are quick to suggest that such dreams are a natural reaction to the trauma of losing someone you care deeply about; an attempt by our minds to offer some kind of pain relief. I can understand this viewpoint but I have come to believe that dreams of departed loved ones are messages of love and support from the world of spirit. I believe this because of unmistakably real dreams I have had of my departed mother and because of the remarkable similarities I have found in the countless letters and emails from people who have also had this type of dream. There are clear distinguishing features of parting or good-bye dreams.

First of all, in the majority of cases the loved one who has passed typically enters a realistic setting, such as the dreamer's bedroom, and starts talking to them. There is also typically no plot, story or theme in the dream. The loved one simply comes in and talks. Again, this is not typical as most dreams consist of more than someone talking. As pointed out previously, the dreamer also feels overwhelmingly that the spiritual experience was real and that they have actually been with a loved one. The personality of the loved one is so instantly recognizable that the dreamer awakes with no doubt in their mind.

Think of all the dreams you have had of other people. You do not usually have a sense that you have actually been visited by them.

Most people also say that dreams of the recently departed are hugely comforting. In my experience people grieving the loss of a loved one are often in a swirl of emotion, making it all the more likely that the uplifting message has come from the world of spirit. So, if you have had a dream of a departed loved one and it has some of the characteristics mentioned above, don't dismiss it as a normal part of the grieving process or wishful thinking. I believe it could well be a message of love and reassurance from beyond the grave.

Flash-forwards

Not only have I come to believe that night visions can transcend the gap between this life and the next and connect us to departed loved ones, I also believe they can bridge the gap between past, present and future and space and time. Such night visions offering tantalizing glimpses of the future are called precognitive dreams or, as I prefer to call them, flash-forwards.

But how can you tell the difference between a precognitive night vision and a dream that should be interpreted symbolically? For example, if you had a dream where you were falling out of a building, should this be interpreted symbolically as fear of failure or will you actually fall out of a building in the future? Flash-forwards have certain hallmarks setting them apart from other dreams. Dreams that should be interpreted symbolically tend to be a series of unconnected surreal images, a bit like watching a music video, whereas flash-forwards tend to be vivid and real and include entire stories or events with a beginning, middle and end.

Bear in mind that flash-forwards that are exact indications of the future are extremely rare. This isn't to say they don't happen. There is plenty of evidence to suggest that they do; for example, a number of people reported having dreams of towers and planes before the 9/11 disaster. More common, though, are flash-forwards offering glimpses of potential futures, or situations that could occur. Although they may not be as dramatic in their accuracy, they are no less remarkable because they give the dreamer an opportunity to experiment with potential courses of action or preview the outcome if a certain course of action is followed. I believe the angels send us such dreams to give us greater information so that we are better equipped to make choices, overcome challenges that lie ahead and make positive changes, if the future we glimpse isn't to our liking. In other words, most flash-forwards suggest possibilities, showing that the future is not fixed and we all have the power to change the outcome of our lives for the better.

One of the most stunning types of flash-forwards is receiving messages from unborn children. About two years ago Gloria wrote to me about a dream she had had about her daughter. In her dream her daughter was proudly holding twin baby boys in her arms and on their T-shirts were the names – Jake and Jonas. Gloria decided not to tell her daughter about this dream because she was on her third cycle of IVF treatment and the outlook wasn't good. But two weeks later she got a call from her daughter telling her that she was pregnant. Seven months later she gave birth to twin baby boys. They were a few weeks premature but otherwise healthy. Gloria never discussed names with her daughter because right up until the babies were born they were afraid of losing them and didn't want to tempt fate. She could not believe it when her daughter told her that they were going to call the boys Jake and Jonas.

Years before my son was conceived, I truly believe I met him in my dreams. He helped me climb up a mountain. Then later everything about his appearance – brown eyes, olive skin and plucky 'can do' personality – turned out to be true. I've had many more unborn children stories like this sent and I've never had any reason to doubt their credibility. Whenever I read them I am reminded again of the wonderful ways angels can reach out to us in our dreams. Our consciousness is not limited to our physical bodies and we all have the ability to communicate across the physical boundaries of space and time.

Embracing Angels in Your Dreams

I think my fascination with dreams probably started when I first saw *The Wizard of Oz* as a young child. I remember going to bed and hoping to be transported to such a magical place. Regretfully, I didn't manage to recreate Oz, but I have managed to visit some remarkable places in my dreams. I've met my departed mother and angels in my dreams and these night visions have convinced me that spirits and angels can reach out to us through the medium of dreams.

Lucid Dreaming

Most of us lose ourselves in our dreams, but there are individuals who have a very different experience when they dream. These people somehow manage to awaken their sense of self in their dreams and become aware that they are dreaming. This experience is called lucid dreaming and holds incredible opportunities for the dreamer to explore the world of dreams and understand the messages hidden there.

Lucid dreaming simply means being aware that you are dreaming. The ability to 'wake up' in your dream and take control of it is rare, but this does not mean it is impossible. If you follow the simple techniques below you have all the tools you need to create your own virtual reality where you can experience anything from flying to travelling into space, from talking to animals to swimming with sharks. Imagine a world created by you where you can do or be anything that you want to be; where you can learn new skills or improve old ones and find creative solutions to just about anything, and where the limitations of waking life just don't exist. It's not just excitement, education and adventure that lucid dreaming has to offer, however.

Lucid Dreaming Techniques

There are many things we do during the day that we will also do in our dreams. For example, meeting someone, or looking at our watch, or catching a bus or train or plane, so during the day get into the habit of asking yourself repeatedly if you are dreaming or are awake. In this way you will be linking the waking act with the dreaming symbol. With practice, if it happens enough, you will automatically remember to ask yourself if you are dreaming in your dreams and will discover that you are.

Before you go to bed think about what you really want to dream about. Repeat the idea or scene in your head.

During your dream visualization imagine yourself using the reality checks you used during the day and becoming lucid. For example, say to yourself, every time I see food in a dream or walk through a door I will become lucid in my dream. Keep thinking about your dream until you fall asleep. In this way you will drift off to that rehearsal and hopefully something might come along in your dream to remind you that you are dreaming. You can take over from there.

Finally, some experts recommend changing your sleep pattern to encourage lucid dreaming; for example, waking up at 4 a.m. and then going back to sleep at 6 a.m. I wouldn't recommend this technique on days when you are working or driving or operating machinery and so on, but it seems that during periods of delayed sleep we tend to have more rapid eye movement or REM sleep – the stage when dreaming occurs – than when we sleep at our normal time.

Lucid dreaming just seems to click with some people, but don't worry if you can't make it happen. Remember, stress and tension create barriers between you and your angels. Perhaps you are more suited to psychic vision in your waking rather than dreaming life. Lucid dreaming is very exciting and a wonderful way to boost your creativity and confidence in your psychic powers, but there are two other types of night visions that have me convinced that we are more than our physical bodies.

Out of Body Experiences (OBEs) and Near Death Experiences (NDEs)

Out of body experiences and near death experiences are often thought to be one and the same, but although there are similarities there are also differences.

An out of body experience typically involves a sensation of floating above your body when you are asleep. Surveys suggest that one in ten people has an out-of-body experience at some time in their lives and those who have experienced them sometimes claim to have observed details unknown to them beforehand. Some people argue that OBEs are nothing more than dreams but to anyone who has ever had one – and I know from correspondence that there are thousands of you – it is so much more than a dream. It is a night vision, a spiritual awakening.

Lisa sent me this story and I'd like to share it with you.

High Above

I had come back from the cinema with my boyfriend and just as he dropped me off at home he told me he wanted to break up with me. We'd been together for three years and he had been my whole world. I couldn't imagine life without him. It broke my heart. I wanted to die literally. I cried myself to sleep that night and at some point after I fell asleep exhausted, I 'awoke' to find myself floating above my body.

I saw that I had fallen asleep with my daytime clothes still on. I noticed all the tissues stained with my tears lying on the bed and the floor around my bed. I floated out of the bedroom, into the bathroom where I floated above the sink, looking into the mirror but saw nothing. Next, I floated into the kitchen and then I floated out of the window and into the street. I knew I was going to visit my boyfriend. I floated into his house and into his bedroom and saw him sleeping soundly. I didn't feel anything for him. There was no connection between us. I knew then that we were not meant to be together. Then, I went back to my house and slipped back into my body.

The next morning I woke up with red eyes and a heavy head but my heart was light. My family and friends couldn't believe how cheerful I was. They had all gathered around to support me but as grateful as I was for their concern I knew that I would be just fine, and I was. My out of body experience was so comforting and uplifting. It helped me realize that I didn't need a boyfriend to feel good about myself. I could be wonderful and magical on my own.

Equally awe-inspiring are stories of people who have visited the afterlife and seen bright lights, angels and spirits of departed loved ones but not died. Typically these near death experiences happen when a person is close to death or when their life expectancy is uncertain, hence the term 'near death experience'. Like OBEs the near death experience is much more common than you think. Some people argue that NDEs are hallucinations or tricks of the mind, but for those who have experienced them they are clear proof that there is an afterlife. Oliver is in no doubt that his NDE changed his mind and his life.

Head-on Collision

I didn't believe in an afterlife before I 'died'. Indeed, if anyone had told me the story I am telling you, I don't think I would have believed them. Anyway here goes:

Back in 1997 I was involved in a head-on collision with another car. My body was thrown with such force through the front window of my car that I landed feet away from the scene of the accident. It took the paramedics a while to pick out the glass stuck in my legs and arms and there were problems carrying me on the stretcher, as I'm a big man. I know all this not because the paramedics told me but because I saw it all happen. I saw it happen without my glasses – they disappeared in the crash – in spirit my vision was so sharp.

I didn't feel any pain. I just saw my lifeless body. There was no sense of attachment to it. I had this feeling that I needed to leave so I didn't linger long at the scene. I started to move into different dimensions. I became transparent and the light surrounding me was intense and radiant. Images of my birth and my life flashed in front of me. I met this woman dressed in white – I think she might have been an angel – who guided me through some tunnels. I think I died at some point. The only way I can compare it is like the feeling you have when you have been on your feet all day and you kick off your shoes in front of the TV. I shall never forget the feeling of relief and comfort and love that surrounded me or the joy that ran through me. How can I describe being protected and hugged by an angel? It is beyond description in human words.

For a while I lost myself in the rapture but then I had this overwhelming feeling that I was being dragged back to the physical. I didn't want to go. I had touched brilliance. I knew that everyone and everything is connected, *always and for ever to the light. How could I return after this glimpse of possibility, but return I did with visions of the afterlife. My life has never been the same again.*

Much as I want to, there isn't space in this book to cover OBEs and NDEs in greater detail, but I'd like to mention that in the vast majority of cases people who have had these experiences are left with a lingering sense of wonder, awe and magic. Many lose their fear of death. There is no doubt in their minds that angels of love and light watch over us in this life and wait for us in the next.

Spirits of Departed Loved Ones

It's an oversimplification, of course, but modern physics tells us that everything – you, me, your house and this book – is made up of energy. The universe is made up of vibrating strings of energy, and how this energy vibrates defines how it manifests in the world. As our bodies and our minds and thoughts are energy, is it so unfeasible then to think that when we die the energy of our thoughts and our hearts can survive in another dimension of reality? And is it possible for this energy to interact with us here on earth?

When we die we leave our physical bodies behind, but our spirits, our energy, lives on, and, when there is a strong connection between people who know and love each other, it is this part of us that can reach back into the physical world. Sometimes the spirits may appear to look as they did when they were alive, typically healthier and more radiant, or they may manifest through a night vision, or a voice, or a feeling, or a sign that a loved one is close by.

Many people have written to say that they have been visited by a departed loved one in spirit form and in most cases these loving spirits have appeared to comfort, guide and protect. It can happen in different ways: in familiar sounds and scents, in unexplained gifts, in dreams, in coincidences or even full-blown apparitions. The stories are positive and show the ways our loved ones can reach out to us without a medium or a psychic.

Often spirits of the departed come back to say 'goodbye', if saying goodbye wasn't possible when they died. These days not being with someone when they die is a common regret as more and more of us live distances apart. I certainly blamed myself when I wasn't able to be with my mum in her final moments, but when my mum finally reached out to me through dreams and an inner voice, I realized how futile and unnecessary my feelings of guilt and regret had been. Not only had my mother tuned into my thoughts and feelings on this, she reassured me that she had made the choice to die alone deliberately because it was easier for her to leave her physical body behind without my presence willing her to stay.

Sometimes spirits of loved ones appear to warn us of impending danger or to give specific advice, but generally it seems our loved ones simply want to let us know they are safe and at peace, that this life is temporary and we will all meet again in heaven. They want to reassure us that we are not alone and are being watched over from the other side. And to let us to know they are proud of us.

Departed loved ones can appear in our dreams, and, for those who are receptive, in full-blown visions, but they may also manifest their presence through angel signs or calling cards. I've listed below the most common ways this can happen. You notice many of these resemble angel calling cards or signs:

- *Feathers*: I get a lot of letters from people about white feathers appearing at significant moments to reassure them that their loved one is close by.

- *Music*: Spirits can impress their energy on a song or piece of music so that you think about them when it is played.

- *Objects*: You may find that holding clothing or objects belonging to a lost loved one can trigger images, thoughts or feelings.

- *Clocks*: Clocks or watches may stop working for no obvious reason.

- *Telephone*: You may hear the phone ringing but when you pick it up no one is there.

- *Electrical appliances*: Radios, TVs and other electrical appliances may stop or start for no reason when no one is around them. Spirits have also been known to scramble images on television or computer screens.

- *Lights*: You may notice that lights flicker or that new light bulbs burn out instantly.

- *Smells*: A common way spirits try to get our attention is scent. You may suddenly become aware of the faint smell of a flower or cigar or familiar perfume and these scents are associated with people who have passed over.

- *Animals*: Sometimes spirit beings will influence a bird or animal to get our attention in some way.

- *Silent shadows*: Unexplained shadows glimpsed in the corner of the eye. You may also experience a feeling of being watched but when you turn around no one is there.

- *Unexplained noises*: Footsteps; knocks, banging, rapping; scratching sounds; sounds of something being dropped. Sometimes these noises can be subtle and other times they can be quite loud.

- *Gust of wind: You* may experience a draught, blast of fresh air or a breath of air on your face.

- *Thoughts and feelings*: Every time you call on your departed loved one with your mind and your heart they are with you in spirit.

Like angels, spirits of loved ones try to get our attention in many ways; you just need to start noticing them. It's a wonderful development that increasing numbers of people are prepared to talk openly about their belief in life after death. The more people open their minds to the idea, the more experiences seem to occur because the spirits understand that it is safe for them to do so.

Indeed, just reading this book will let them know that your understanding of life and death is changing and growing and that you may be ready for contact, or signs of 'life' from the other side. The key word here, though, is 'ready'. The spirits will only reveal themselves when you are ready.

Working through Grief

When someone you love dies the pain can be gut-wrenching and unbearable, especially if you are overwhelmed with feelings of regret, wondering if there was something you could or should have said and done. Although you can't physically touch, cry or laugh with them any more, I hope this book will show you that you can experience them in a different way. They can stay alive in your heart and in your mind and be with you more intensely than ever before.

As I know from bitter experience, working through grief to the point where you can experience them and reunite with them in spirit is easier said than done. Many people ask why they can't sense their loved one around them or when they should expect signs from them. My answer is always the same – spirits of departed loved ones can communicate with us immediately after passing; there are no limits of time in the world of spirit, and they are as eager to reach us as we are to reach them. The issue, however, is not with the spirits but with *us*.

Before spirits can make contact with us there needs to be a period of acceptance of the passing first. It is truly wonderful when a departed loved one returns in spirit but as amazing as this contact is it cannot bring them back. Once you have been able to come to terms with the physical loss, and feel strong enough emotionally, spirits of departed loved ones are more likely to appear. They find it hard to break through when feelings of anger and desperation close down our minds and our hearts and cannot make contact unless you are in the right frame of mind.

How Can This Frame of Mind Be Achieved?

The first and only step is to experience the grief. A loved one has died and the pain created by the loss has created an emotional wound that needs to heal. You need to cry. You need to mourn. For the first few days and weeks after my mother died I didn't mourn and I paid a heavy price for my denial. I was so convinced that my mum was alive in spirit I thought that getting upset would deny my belief in the afterlife. What I didn't realize, and had to learn painfully, was that if I did not allow myself to grieve for the loss, my emotional wound would not heal, and I would be unable to move forward with my life emotionally and spiritually.

I had to learn that grieving the loss of a loved one does not mean you have lost faith in the afterlife, it simply means you are human and missing human contact with someone you love. I had to learn that before the joy of reunion in spirit I needed to go through the pain of grief in much the same way that a mother experiences the pain of labour before the joy of holding a new baby in her arms.

Learning about grief is helpful. Many of us fear grief because it hurts, but even though it won't reduce the pain knowing what is normal and what is not can reduce the fear. Although everyone experiences a deep sense of loss when someone they love dies, no two people respond in exactly the same way.

Initially, the most common response is denial and shock but when the emotional numbness lifts and the reality of the loss hits you may experience a range of confusing emotions such as anger, guilt, helplessness and fear. Anger at being left alone by someone you love is especially confusing but it is very common. Guilt is also common. You may feel you did not do or say the right things before your loved one died. As frightening as these emotions can be, try to remember that these feelings are neither good nor bad, simply feelings. It is what you do with your feelings that make them right or wrong.

If you don't work through these feelings, you may direct anger at others in hurtful ways or become severely depressed. Grief may also produce physical symptoms such as insomnia, headaches, fatigue and stomach upsets which you could consult your doctor about. A counsellor may be able to help you talk through your feelings, if you don't feel you can open up to a friend or a family member.

Although there are common responses to grief we all vary widely with respect to the length of time that we grieve. Some people move quickly through the stages of grief, while others may grieve on and off for months and years. There are no rights or wrongs when it comes to this but you need to give yourself the time that you need. Grieving can't be hurried. You can't just snap out of it or get over it. Just as it takes time to heal broken bones, it takes time for broken hearts to heal.

In short, to move through grief and emerge a healthy and happy person you must give yourself the time to experience the emotions associated with it. There are no quick-fix cures to deaden or escape the pain. At times you may wonder if you will ever pull through but you must give in to the healing process. An old Turkish proverb states 'He that conceals his grief finds no remedy for it' and like many proverbs this is very true. Denying your emotions will not destroy them and if you don't let your feelings out they could come out at some other time or in some other way. Remember, it is OK to cry or feel angry. It is OK to scream out loud. You are not losing control – you are reacting to your loss.

It's very important not to isolate yourself from the support of others when you are grieving. If you had a physical wound you would allow others to take care of you, so do the same for your emotional wound. If the help isn't there from family and friends contact your doctor and ask for support. And when you feel ready it can help to return to your daily routine. Search for activities that are meaningful to you; staying productive and keeping in touch with the world around you can give you a sense of purpose as can taking care of yourself physically. Eating healthily, getting adequate sleep and rest, and exercising regularly are all common-sense methods that can help ease your pain.

If you experience a sense of guilt or worthlessness because you are alive and your loved one isn't try not to go there. It was your loved one's time to pass and not yours. You are unique. There is and never will be again another person like you on this wonderful earth, and the world of spirit wants your energy and your spirit to remain here for the time being. There is still a purpose and a destiny for you to fulfil and other people need to see the angel in you. You may feel alone but perhaps one day you will be able to help someone else move through and beyond their grief.

Moving Beyond Your Grief

Working through grief cannot be achieved without pain and hurt. It will take time, sometimes a long time but trust me, because I've lost people I thought I couldn't live without, the pain does fade and there is life beyond death, but it will be a new life for you and a new life for your loved one in spirit.

Trying to get back to 'normal' or 'your old self again' after your loved one has passed isn't something you should aim for because it is an impossible goal. As painful as it may feel, you can't go back to normal. Your life has changed for ever and you will be changed by the loss. Now your choice is – is this change to be a positive or a negative one?

You can celebrate the time you shared with your loved one on earth or you can choose to live in sadness and bitterness. It's obvious which approach the spirit of your departed loved one would prefer you to take. What better memorial to their lives could there be than you remembering them with feelings of joy? Remember, moving through your grief does not mean that you go into denial, or try to forget the person who has died, it means being able to remember without feelings of intense pain stopping you in your tracks.

I want to stress that this takes time. You can't and shouldn't try to hurry up the process. Grief is much like the ebb and flow of the sea – sometimes the waves lap gently on the shore but sometimes they crash hard. With time your pain will ease and you will come to a place where memories of your loved one are gentle and sweet. You will also come to a place when you reclaim a part of yourself.

When you love someone deeply you give a part of yourself away. This 'giving over' of yourself is one of the most beautiful things about love as long as you don't take it to extremes. If too much of your self-worth and happiness is bound to someone else this isn't healthy for them or you because you are confusing love with need. True love, and the most powerful and healing love of all, is the love that can set a spirit free and when a loved one dies amid all the pain your loved one gives you an opportunity to reclaim the part of yourself you gave to them, the creativity and passion that is yours. Clearly this will take time but if you allow yourself to work through your grief you will eventually find that your strength and potential returns to you. You will rediscover who you really are in spirit and there can be nothing more comforting and healing than that.

Entering the World of Spirit

It may be difficult to comprehend but the death of a loved one can lead to a reawakening of your spirit if you allow yourself to fully experience the loss. This is certainly what happened to me. As I outlined in the Introduction, it was only after my mother died that I finally opened to the world of spirit. When I had gone through all the stages of grief all that was left was this overwhelming feeling that the love I had for my mother had not died. This love was still very much alive and it was watching over me from the other side.

There are some rare people who seem to be born with 'angel eyes', and a deep connection to the world of spirit. I wasn't one of those, and I suspect there are many people like me who need some kind of shock to help them see the light. For me the emotional crisis triggered by the loss of my mum opened a psychic door and angels came rushing in. For other people it may not be the loss of a loved one that triggers their spiritual transformation; it may be fear of their own death that triggers a sense of urgency. Or it could be a deeply personal crisis, such as depression or addiction or perhaps a bout of illness, redundancy or a relationship breaking up that forces a re-evaluation of priorities. Or it could be something much less traumatic, like a stunning coincidence, the selfless act of a stranger or the desire to help others which is the trigger for the realization that there has to be more to this life than the physical.

Whatever the crisis or trigger is for you, rest assured when you are ready it will call out to you loud and clear, and it will keep calling out to you until you listen. So, if you don't think you have heard or seen your angels yet, be patient, in time you will. Perhaps there is more for your soul to learn and experience before they reveal themselves to you. Don't try to rush or pressure yourself.

Just live your life with goodness, love and integrity. This doesn't mean trying to be perfect – again that is impossible, because to be human is to be imperfect – it means doing the best you can and living in a way that you feel your guardian angel would approve.

Remember, even if you can't always see, hear or feel them, whether you are eight or eighty your angels are always watching you and always calling out to you. They will wait patiently for you until you are ready to hear and see them.

PART FIVE

Everyday Miracles

*Join in on the movement and
go out and do a random act of kindness.
Then say, 'My angel made me do it.'*

Sally Sharp

If you would like to see magic in the ordinary and wonder in the commonplace, this section has been written for you. It begins with a discussion of some of the ways angels can work their magic in everyday life, and how inviting that magic into your life can benefit your health, your relationships, your career and all aspects of your life. You also learn something many people don't know – angels have a sense of humour. Then we move on to discuss mysterious strangers or people who seem to appear out of nowhere to offer assistance or aid and then vanish afterwards. Also we'll look at other guises angels can use to manifest or express themselves, most notably children and animals, before concluding with an important discussion about the phenomenon of aspiring or earthbound angels, and whether or not you may be one.

What Is a Miracle?

For most of us when the word 'miracle' comes to mind, we think of something like the parting of the Red Sea. Our notion of the miraculous still comes from very ancient sources, like the Old Testament. Some people believe in these miracles in a literal sense, while others believe them to be inspiring stories or allegories. Others think they could be true, but if they are, they happened in the distant past; these things just don't happen today. But miracles aren't just confined to ancient times, or bestowed only upon those who are 'chosen'. They are happening to ordinary people every day.

The dictionary defines a miracle as: 'An event that appears inexplicable by the laws of nature and so is held to be supernatural in origin or an act of God.' Although a divine origin cannot be proved, what we do know is that unexplained incidents happen all the time.

A woman wakes up in the middle of the night with a vivid dream fresh in her mind. In her dream she saw her sister smiling happily and waving goodbye as she walks up a large and magnificent staircase towards a blinding, white light. The next morning she gets a phone call from her sister's husband saying that her sister passed away unexpectedly in the night with a heart attack.

A man sees a boy fall from a wall as he is walking down the street. The boy's arm is broken, so he takes the boy to hospital. When mother and son are reunited at the hospital, the man recognizes her as a former girlfriend. They start dating again, fall in love, and eventually get married. On their wedding night the woman tells the man that the boy he helped is, in fact, his son.

A family move house, from the countryside to the city.
They leave their cat in the care of neighbours, thinking
the cat will be happier in the country than in the city.
Three months later the cat manages to travel over forty
miles to find them.

All these stories are incredible, amazing, little short of miraculous when you read them. Yet, they are all true. Plenty of people try to explain them away as astonishing coincidences. I often wonder why so many of us are afraid of using the word 'miracle'. It's possible that many of us in this scientific age are apprehensive about using the word 'miracle' because of its strong links to religion, but miracles are also for those with a scientific approach to life, because science, in its purest sense, is the search for truth. And the search for truth must include all possibilities, including the possibility of miracles.

Everyday miracles may not always be dramatic, like the parting of the Red Sea. Sometimes they are just small blessings or unexplained coincidences or gifts. Yet, they are all part of the same miraculous power connecting all things. Viewed in this light I don't think miracles are a matter of religion, or indeed belief. I think they are a matter of *recognition*. Just look around you and within you. Think about the miracle of your life. Consider the incredible experiences of other people, like those who submitted stories for this book. The more we acknowledge the wonder in our everyday lives, the easier it is for us to believe in the reality of miracles.

And Why Not Believe in Miracles?

When confronted with the unknown or inexplicable we have a clear choice. We can ignore it, or explain it away as chance, or a stroke of good luck, or we can choose to interpret it as something meaningful and important. Since you are in control of what you think, feel and believe, why not believe in something that gives you greater hope? Why not believe in wonder? Why not believe that things are not always what they seem? Why not find magic in the ordinary? Why not believe in angels?

Why not ask your angels to help you in all areas of your life? If you open your mind and your heart to them, they can help protect you and guide you with your career and relationships. They can help put you in the right place at the right time, and place helpful people in your path. They can help calm you, heal you and inspire you to stretch your own boundaries. All you need to know is that they are here to help you and all you need to do is ask them.

Career

If you feel you need a change of career, ask your angels every day to help you. Remember, you don't necessarily need to meditate or light candles. You don't even need to call out loud to them, just talk to them with your thoughts and feelings. Before you ask for their help, you may want to write down what it is that you want to happen first. The clearer you are in your mind about this, the easier it is for your celestial guides to help you. Keep asking them and then look out for signs and messages from them. For example, you may notice a training course that interests you, or meet someone who offers you advice, or overhear something on the television or radio that pulls you in the direction of the place you need to go.

It was an overheard conversation that gave me the career break I needed. At the time I was fresh out of university and soon joined the ranks of the unemployed. I wasn't sure what I wanted to do with my life, but I knew it had something to do with books and publishing, so I applied for the position of editorial assistant in numerous publishing houses. The rejections came thick and fast and I started to wonder if I would ever get a job. Then one day, after yet another dismal job interview, I missed my train home by about two minutes. How I cursed when the train drew out of the station just as I arrived. Now I would have to wait for an hour on a cold station – in those days stations didn't have as many coffee shops and facilities as they do now. I was also hungry but didn't have enough money to buy anything, so feeling sorry for myself I sat down on a chair and began to question whether or not publishing was in fact the career for me.

After a few moments the delicious smell of fish and chips filled the air. I realized that a couple of guys were sitting behind me enjoying a feast. They were talking quite loudly and I overheard that they were students from the London School of Printing and Publishing and were, like me, applying for jobs in the industry. I heard one of them say he had an interview the following morning at Unwin Hyman books. I also heard him laugh, and say he would have to do some reading up tonight, because he didn't know anything about 'New Age mumbo jumbo' as the job involved working on astrology and psychic development books. My ears pricked up and the next morning I called up the publishing house and got myself an interview. Needless to say, I didn't need to do any reading up – I was an expert already – and I got the job and never looked back or doubted my career choice since.

I often wonder if I had caught that train whether or not I would be where I am today. I think of it as my 'Sliding Doors' moment, in homage to the movie starring

Gwyneth Paltrow. There is a school of thought that believes nothing that happens to us, even something as apparently trivial as missing a train, is an accident. Whether or not this is true I don't know, but I do know that giving reverence and respect to every moment of your life, however seemingly unimportant or trivial, because it could potentially be life-changing, is a fulfilling and happy way to live. The more we are able to focus our full attention on the deep meaning and potential of the present, the greater our chances of creating a wonderful future for ourselves.

Another thing that your angels can do to assist you with your career is to help you be true to yourself. If you are waking up each morning before work with a sense of dread because you hate your job, keep asking them to help you make a change. The key word here is 'you'. Remember, your heavenly guides won't take away your free will and do everything for you, but they can help fill you with a sense of purpose and passion. So often when people make the wrong career choices, or feel stuck as far as their career is concerned, it is because they feel they aren't in control of their lives. The angels can help you see that you are in control. You can make decisions for yourself. Sometimes making changes will be tough, and you will need discipline and patience to follow them through, but the important thing is that you are in the driving seat.

If you aren't sure what work you should be doing, experiment until you find one you love. In this day and age the old concept of one career for life is fast disappearing and many of us will retrain and switch. As far as I am concerned this is all positive because every life path you choose is an opportunity for learning and growing. And at the end of the day, it isn't your career success that your angels are paying attention to, but how much you have learned and grown spiritually along the way. Remember, nobody on their deathbed says, 'I wish I had spent more time at the office.'

Wealth

Who isn't struggling to pay the bills or keep up financially these days? We are living through a recession, after all. Is it possible then to ask your angels to help you make ends meet?

It certainly is and sometimes they will help and you may find yourself presented with unexpected gifts of money. However, your angels don't work in this way because in the world of spirit money has no significance. That's why praying to them to help you win the Lottery or a windfall doesn't work. They aren't interested in money, they are only interested in you. If financial concerns are causing stress they can help by giving you the motivation to make the important decision to live within your means. They may also inspire you to seek new sources of income or get access to financial advice or get organized with your bills and invoices and so on. Often simple organizational changes are all that is needed and your angels can help with that.

Love

I get so many letters asking me if angels can help them find a life partner or soulmate. Love and romance are a huge source of happiness and fulfilment so, of course, the angels can help. In rare cases they will intervene directly if you ask them for help in matters of the heart, by placing someone in your life at the right place and right time. It can help to be specific when you ask your angels for a partner. Write down the qualities you want in a future partner and don't sell yourself short. You really do deserve the best. More typically, though, your angels will not intervene directly but help by encouraging you to discover things about yourself that you love. The reason they help in this way is because they know that unless you can fall in love with yourself first, you can never experience fulfilling love for another person.

If you don't like yourself, how can you like, love and take care of someone else? So, if you are looking for love and romance the place to start is wherever you are. Treat yourself as if you were the most special person in the world. Be tolerant with your failings, as you would be tolerant of a lover's failings. Take good care of yourself. Encourage yourself to be the best that you can be, as you would encourage someone you love. Seek out interests and hobbies that make your heart sing. I promise you that if you take the focus away from seeking a mate and place it more on making yourself feel fulfilled and happy, love will find you.

Sometimes this love will take the form of self-love, and by this I don't mean a selfish, self-centred existence, I mean living with respect and gratitude for the miracle of your existence. You may find that you are perfectly happy without a partner, because you know that the love of your angels in heaven and your friends on earth is enough to sustain you. Or this love may take the form of a union between like-minded souls. Neither life choice is better or worse as far as your angels are concerned. All that matters is whether or not the choices you make in love and life are ones that bring you inner peace.

Health

If you suffer from health problems or find it hard to diet or exercise, asking your angels for help can be a good idea.

I struggled with bouts of depression in my teens and again in my early thirties, and I am in no doubt that asking your angels for help can bring healing and lightness. I've also been sent remarkable stories of people who have been healed by angels and in my book *An Angel Healed Me* I collected a large number of these together. Some of these healings took place during great physical or emotional illness, while others concern the terminally ill and dying, and for many even the doctors involved say the only explanation has to be the existence of a higher power.

This is not to say that anyone who is ill can simply pray to their angels and get better. For reasons we may never understand while we are still human, sometimes the angels will intervene to ease suffering and sometimes they will not. However, even when there appears to be no physical respite, opening your mind and heart to your angels can help make any suffering easier to bear. It is spiritual healing, or healing from the inside out, rather than healing from the outside in, that is the greatest gift from your angels.

Protection

The traditional role of your guardian angel is one of protection and safe-keeping. It is comforting to know that you are never alone. Our celestial guides can't always keep us safe from danger, but from many 'angel saved my life' stories it is clear that sometimes they do.

Why angels protect lives on some occasions and not others is a mystery that we cannot understand in this life. Yet when I look at the stories I have been sent, and compare them with my own experiences, I think in the great majority of cases it is a clear and loud inner voice that is the decisive factor. There is a moment when the person involved has the choice of following that inner voice or ignoring it. The lesson to be learned from this is that if you do hear a strong inner voice telling you to do something or take action, you may want to listen to it.

Angels can protect us from physical danger, but their chief concern is to bring us hope and comfort when we feel alone or in emotional distress. So often people grieving tell me that in the midst of their grief they unexpectedly felt an invisible warmth or presence that they could not explain and this gave them tremendous comfort. It could be an invisible hand on the shoulder, an unseen kiss or the simple feeling of being given a warm and loving hug. In many cases, when these incidents occurred the person had switched off their mind in some way. Perhaps they were drifting off to sleep, or standing in a queue or doing routine chores. It seems the angels find it easier to reach out and take away our fears when we let our minds relax.

Day-to-day Tasks

Don't make the mistake of thinking your angels will only reach out to you in times of crisis or turmoil. They can help you with every aspect of your life including things you might consider trivial such as finding lost objects, locating a parking space or deciding which clothes to buy. Your celestial guardians are there to help you whenever you call on them and they will help you feel happy and protected.

Spiritual and Personal Growth

The fact that you are reading this book is proof enough for your angels that you are in tune with the idea that there is more to this life than meets the eye. I hope it will also have encouraged you to connect with the angel within you and take charge of your life.

If this book has inspired you to look within, then your spiritual journey has already begun and in the days to follow you will discover more and more ways to connect with your spiritual self. You will find yourself drawn through your intuition and developing psychic senses to people, things, books, events and ideas that will guide, heal and inspire you.

How will you know when you are on this spiritual journey? The answer is simple: you will find more and more reasons to smile. As your heart opens up to your angels, laughter and feelings of joy will re-enter your life.

Sense of Humour

Recall that famous Chesterton quote 'Angels can fly because they take themselves lightly'? Many people think of angels being very serious, but there is reason to believe that they take themselves lightly. We don't have difficulty thinking of angels as comforting and reassuring us, so wouldn't it follow that they also have a sense of humour?

I have many amusing stories about angels. Ringtones going off at inappropriate times and defusing overly serious situations is very common. I had one lovely story sent to me about a wedding where everyone was very nervous. So nervous you could have cut the atmosphere with a knife. The bride's sister desperately wanted everyone to relax and enjoy themselves on this special day, but things went from bad to worse when there was a mix-up with the cake orders and the wrong cake delivered. However, as the final vows were about to be taken the bride's sister got her wish for smiles and laughter. The vicar had forgotten to turn off his phone and a 'Crazy Frog' theme tune burst out loud and clear. Just as funny was the fact that around a third of those present reached for their phones thinking the ringtone came from their phone. When the culprit was discovered laughter and light-heartedness replaced any tension and nerves.

Sometimes we are all guilty of taking ourselves too seriously, but the angels are never closer to us than when we have fun experiences. Look back on your life, and think about funny moments, and how often they have been the most memorable times. Humour is a powerful tool for spiritual and personal growth and we should all use it more. Life can be serious but it can also be very funny. Angels are serious about their role of protecting us, but this doesn't mean they can't have fun doing it. Laugh along with them.

Angel Children

Children, like angels, love to laugh. They laugh up to four hundred times a day, in comparison to adults, who only average about fifteen. If you ever need to give your faith in angels a boost, talk to young children. They are fresh from heaven and have the innocence and trust to see the miraculous and look all around them with wonder and open-mindedness. Don't dismiss it all as imagination. A child's open-mindedness means not shutting out things that don't conform to logic or reason, and it is this ability to suspend doubt which makes them more receptive to angel visitations. Sadly, as we get older, doubt and fear tend to replace this trust and acceptance and we stop seeing the miraculous in everyone and everything.

Watching children listen to their angels can remind us to listen to our own. How they accept readily and don't question what they see. They talk about angels in such a matter-of-fact way, without any doubt that what they are experiencing is real. Could anything be more simple and obvious than this lovely email sent to me by Carl's mother, Rachael?

Copying

As soon as my three-year-old son Carl told me about his angel I just knew I had to get in touch with you. I was giving him his bath when he started splashing his hands up and down in the water. I asked him what he was doing and he said he was 'copying'. I asked him who he was copying and he gave me one of his 'dah' or isn't it just obvious looks and pointed to high up on the wall in front of him. I looked at the wall and couldn't see anything. I didn't tell my son this though and smiled and waved.

'She like that, my lady with wings like that!' he shouted, splashing his arms even faster up and down.

This is another charming little angel child story, sent to me by Anne Marie.

So Pretty

This story was told to my daughter by her husband, who heard it from his friend. The friend, a young man, had taken his daughter to an open-air concert organized by a church or churches on, I think, Brighton beach. He had his four-year-old daughter on his shoulders, and she said 'Daddy, can you see all the angels in the sky floating above the people, they are so pretty!' The young man and his wife couldn't see anything, but the child spent the whole time looking up at the sky at the angels and talking about them.

Many parents write asking if I think their child is making it up, and I tell them the best way to determine if it is a true angel experience is the child's response. Is the child unsettled in any way? If there is fear or panic then the experience is not typically angel-based, and may be more to do with attention-seeking or too much exposure to frightening images on television. But if the child is matter of fact, like Carl, and feels safe or even entertained by the experience, then I believe it to be genuine.

Young children generally find it very comforting to know that their guardian angel is by their side. I always tell my children before they go to sleep that angels are watching over them making sure they don't have any bad dreams. I encourage my children to talk to their angels every night and thank them for their guidance, even if they can't always see them. I'd encourage other parents to do the same. Sadly, many adults react with doubt and suspicion whenever a child talks about what they can see and sense from the world of spirit and this can cause confusion for the child. They start to doubt themselves, and the more they doubt their ability to see magic all around them, the less they are able to see.

Is it naive and childish to believe in angels? No, I don't believe it is, because the more we encourage our children to stay young at heart, and the more we get in touch with the child in each one of us, the more we can move forward from 'grown up' fear and self-doubt and start noticing angels all around us.

So, even if you can't see what they are seeing, if your child or the child of someone you know talks to you about seeing or hearing angels encourage them to talk about their experiences. Encourage them to stay receptive to the world of magic, wonder and possibility. Children today urgently need to stay open to the message of love and goodness the angels bring to counteract the upsetting messages of injustice and violence that seem to have become a part of everyday life. All children need to understand that even though angels can't solve the world's problems, trusting in them can give a much-needed sense of comfort and hope.

Animal Angels

In much the same way that children can teach us spiritual lessons, about being open to the wonder all around us and within us, I believe animals can teach us important spiritual lessons about compassion, empathy, healing and the power of unconditional love.

Many letters have come from people with incredible stories like this one, sent to me by Chloe about her dog, Cuba.

Cuba

My dog saved my life. I'm in no doubt of that. I wouldn't be writing to you today without him. I fell asleep after a night out with my friends forgetting that I had left the stove on. The house filled with smoke but I had no idea because I was a little drunk and worse for wear. Thank goodness Cuba managed to rouse me with her frantic barking and jumping on me. She's amazing.

This isn't the only time she has saved my life. When I was in my late teens I got very depressed. I'd spend days in bed wishing I would disappear. My family tried everything to help me but for almost a year I was in another place. Then my sister's husband came home one day with this gorgeous puppy and told me he wanted me to look after it because nobody else had the time. At first I didn't want to but he told me that if I didn't the dog would probably have to be put down. I know now he was bluffing but at the time I believed him. Cuba looked so helpless and afraid my heart went out to her and I took care of her. Suddenly, my life had a routine again. I had to get out and take her for walks, to the vet. I had to make sure she was well cared for. I had to take the focus off myself and put some of it on her and it was the best medicine in the world. Within months I was getting the pieces of my life back together – with Cuba by my side I was ready to live again.

Then there are remarkable stories like that of Faith the biped dog. This courageous Labrador–chow mix was born without front legs. Eight years after her birth, the little yellow dog zips around crowded shops, bustling along with confidence. Since her first steps in March 2003, Faith has been a regular guest on American talk shows and a huge hit on YouTube. She has also become a symbol of hope for injured soldiers. Fans of the little dog say she provides inspiration because she shows us all that different can be beautiful, that it is not the body you are in but the soul that you have.

I've had stories sent to me about the spirits of animals who continue to visit their owners from the other side. I don't doubt this because I believe my beloved cat, Crystal, visited me in spirit. After Crystal died at the respectable age of eighteen, I would often wake up in the night crying because I missed her so much. I would doze back to sleep convinced she was snuggling close to me, as she always used to. I remember one night being absolutely sure she was in bed with me. I switched on the light and when I looked down there was a football-sized dent on the bed where I had felt her. (And no, before you jump to conclusions there wasn't anyone else with me at the time!)

Initially, I dismissed Crystal's nocturnal visit as wishful thinking, but when the experience occurred again the following night I knew that something very 'real' was happening. I had just climbed into bed and heard Crystal's reassuring purr and felt the brush of her whiskers across my cheek. Then I felt little paws padding on my stomach before they settled in the spot where Crystal always used to sleep. I felt the weight of her body pressing against me even though when I glanced down there was no cat there. I didn't want to move a muscle, because I didn't want the sensation to end. The next morning there was no sign that Crystal had visited me, but I knew that she had come back to offer me closure and comfort when I needed it most.

It's not only pets that are touched by angels, but all creatures great and small. I hear many stories about angels using wild animals, birds, butterflies, ladybirds and even insects to communicate messages of love from the world of spirit. Love is the most powerful force in the universe, and whether that love is for a human or an animal, it cannot be broken by death. Love in whatever shape or form transcends death.

Indeed, animal angel stories could fill a whole book by themselves and I simply can't do justice to them all here. I hope, though, that this has at least opened your mind to the very real possibility that animals can be touched by miracles in the same way humans can or even be 'angels in disguise' themselves.

Our animal companions don't ask much from us. They simply love us, walk with us and watch over us in this life and the next, and even though they may not be angels in the traditional sense, this always sounds a great deal like an angel to me.

Mysterious Strangers

Sometimes everyday miracles can occur through the actions or words of our fellow human beings. In some cases this manifests in the appearance of mysterious strangers who arrive in times of need or crisis, and then seem to mysteriously vanish afterwards, often without waiting for so much as a 'thank you'.

These astonishing things do happen, of course. As I recounted in Part Two, when my son was just eight months old his life was saved by a mysterious young boy who stopped him falling down some stone steps. I can still picture him close to eleven years later. He had jet-black hair, blue eyes and a lopsided kind of smile. I've been told many times that he was very likely a child who came along at the right time to do a good deed, but in my street children that young didn't wander around on their own, and how on earth did he vanish so quickly afterwards when I turned away for just the briefest of moments to hug my son? Human or divine, it doesn't really matter, that child will always be an angel to me.

There is something very compelling about these kinds of human angel stories – and there are always reasons why those who experience them remember their helper as something miraculous. They arrive and disappear virtually unseen. There is something out of this world about their appearance – for example, in the way they dress or look – and they often have the exact tools or remedy needed in a crisis and in some cases they even know things, such as names or places, that they can't possibly know.

If they are indeed celestial helpers, then no further explanation is needed; if they are humans, however, then it is harder to explain them. Are these amazing people consciously or unconsciously guided by the angels within and around them or brought to a situation by a psychic connection? Or, as the parents of four-year-old Benjamin wholeheartedly believe, after their son's life was miraculously saved by a passer-by, are they simply 'angels in disguise'?

Benjamin's story was reported to the media, but for those who didn't read it here is a brief summary:

Our Guardian Angel

On 31 July 2009 Benjamin Nelson-West was with his mother, Adrianna, on a Piccadilly Line platform at Acton station in west London. A train drew up and Adrianna got in. Then she began screaming. Benjamin had lost his footing and was stuck in the gap between train and platform. The train doors were starting to close and at that moment Tochukwu Mokah, an engineer from Nigeria waiting for another train, lay down on the platform and put his hands in the gap and pulled the child to safety. After he had passed the boy to his mother, the train pulled out with Mr Mokah still on the platform and Mrs Nelson-West and her son on the train. Everything happened so fast, she didn't even get a chance to say thank you. It took a while to track him down but eventually Mrs Nelson-West managed it and expressed her heartfelt gratitude to her son's 'guardian angel'.

Maureen Lipscombe, a sixty-nine-year-old grandmother, also owes her life to heroic passers-by:

Life Savers

Maureen was hit by a car and left for dead at a pelican crossing on the junction of Lothian Road and the West Approach Road in Edinburgh when Dog's Trust worker Christine Corrigan, thirty-five, and youth worker Kenny Toshack, forty-five, rushed to her aid.

Miss Corrigan said: 'The most horrifying thing was that none of the other cars stopped to help her. It was the week before Christmas and people looked more concerned about doing their Christmas shopping than stopping to help an old woman who was bleeding on the road. I just had to fling myself in front of the traffic to protect her because if I didn't she would have been run over again and again. I'm not normally in the business of saving human lives – I'm more used to caring for animals – but I just did what any human being should do when they see a person in distress.'

Mr Toshack said: 'She was bleeding from her head and face and there was quite a lot of blood, but the cars just kept whizzing past us as we tried to help her. I didn't really think about it. We had a job to do.'

Ambulance crews arrived within half an hour, and told Christine and Kenny that their actions probably saved Mrs Lipscombe's life.

These inspiring stories show that, no matter how it is explained, 'angels in disguise' do seem to be out there, offering the rest of us a much-needed dose of hope and trust in the selflessness of strangers, our fellow human beings. They also show us that we all have the potential to be 'angels in disguise'.

Much of what we hear on the news is upsetting and disturbing, but if you take the time to look you can find inspiring Good Samaritan stories about ordinary people with remarkable selflessness and courage, intervening at just the right time to save a person's life. Even though these people behave like angels they are not angels, but simply ordinary human beings acting with courage.

Whether human or divine, Good Samaritan stories remind us powerfully that angels can also exist within all of us. So, if you don't think you can see angels, one of the best ways to begin seeing them is from the inside out. I am in no doubt that there's potentially an angel in all of us. We can all be aspiring angels offering others simple gestures of love. Although we may not save lives in a dramatic way, and we aren't all in a position to give time and money to good causes, we can all make a difference by bringing comfort and laughter to other people. It doesn't have to be much, simply smiling and saying 'thank you', or paying a compliment, or holding the door open for a stranger, or giving up your seat to someone who needs it can make someone else's day.

If we could all just lose our fear and reach out to one another, and then teach this to our children, imagine the effect it would have on everyone and everything. And if we help our angels to help others, imagine how much easier it would be for everyone to believe in them.

A Glimpse of Heaven

If what you have read so far has struck a familiar chord or moved you in some way, I'm in no doubt the words are speaking to the divine light within you. You may even be what I like to call an aspiring or earthbound angel. I've met many aspiring angels over the years and some of their stories are in this book.

Aspiring angels tend to be extremely sensitive individuals with a strong desire and a gift for inspiring, healing, helping or teaching others, although their own lives may feel difficult as they struggle to reconcile their thirst for spiritual growth with life's daily routines and conventions. People feel they can open up easily to them, yet they themselves may not always find it so easy to open up to others and this can make them feel isolated or somehow different. Alongside all this, there is a powerful sense of purpose, even if they aren't quite sure what that purpose is.

If this sounds a little like you, I am so happy you were guided towards this book, because it was written for and about you. I pray that reading it will be a comfort to you, and help heal any wounds you have suffered over the years for being highly sensitive, or for not easily slotting in to the norms dictated by organizations, religions and expectations. I pray that it will open your mind to the possibility that there are angels all around you and an aspiring angel inside you. I pray that it will help you understand that your sensitivity and creativity is a strong indication of your psychic potential and that your interest in matters spiritual (perhaps criticized by others as 'head in the clouds') isn't your weakness but your greatest strength.

Above all, though, I pray that this book will show you that you do have a purpose – a great and important destiny – and that is to discover and connect with the aspiring angel within you, so that you can become a beacon of hope to others, helping the angels draw closer to earth through their deep connection with you. And once you let go of self-doubt and fear, once you embrace your destiny, heaven will reveal itself to you from the inside out.

So, from now on, whenever you want to catch a glimpse of heaven on earth, whenever you want to see an angel, you could just look in the mirror.

PART SIX

Divine Miscellany

*'I have started to believe there are angels
all around me and it is starting to make
me feel good about living again.'*

Jackie

In my writing career I have often come across wonderful angel-related quotes, anecdotes or information which I file away intending to include in a future book, but then I get carried away with writing, use up my word count and find I can't include them. So, when I was given the go-ahead to include a miscellany at the end of this book I was delighted. Here at last was my chance to include heavenly quotes, stories and other inspirations for my readers. I hope you enjoy reading it as much as I enjoyed pulling it all together.

I've organized everything loosely into two sections – angel words and angel voices – but miscellanies are designed to amaze, amuse and entertain with interesting facts and insights, so just dip into it at your leisure. There's such a mix of angel-inspired ideas you're bound to find something that intrigues or enlightens you.

Angel Words

People often write to me saying how just reading and re-reading a single quote in one of my books – I usually put them at the beginning of each chapter – has encouraged a shift of perspective, or spoken clearly to their hearts. I've noticed how so many of my readers end their letters or emails to me with poignant quotes, so I decided to gather as many of these quotations together. Feel free to use them in your correspondence, share or forward them with someone you care about, or anyone you feel is in need of encouragement, comfort or guidance. If chosen well and used wisely, words have the power to ripple through our souls and change lives.

Below are some of these inspirational angel quotes that I've arranged according to themes relevant to the focus of this book – how to see your angels. Some of them might be very familiar to you, but others you might not have heard of or read before. I will let them speak for themselves and may each and every one bring feelings of magic and comfort to you – and to all those you choose to share them with.

Angel Quotations

Angels: Who and What They Are

All God's angels come to us disguised.
James Russell Lowell

Friends are like angels who lift us to our feet when our wings have trouble remembering how to fly.
Anonymous

*Angels are intelligent reflections of light, that original
light which has no beginning. They can illuminate. They
do not need tongues or ears, for they can communicate
without speech, in thought.*

John of Damascus

*Be not forgetful to entertain strangers, for thereby some
have entertained angels unawares.*

Hebrews, 13:2

*An angel is someone who helps you believe in miracles
again. And that is a friend, lover, child, book, poem, pet
or anyone or anything that makes your heart sing.*

Anonymous

*Angels are the guardians of hope and wonder, the keepers of
magic and dreams. Wherever there is love, an angel is flying
by. Your guardian angel knows you inside and out, and
loves you just the way you are. Angels keep it simple and
always travel light. Remember to leave space in your relationships so the angels have room to play. Your guardian
angel helps you find a place when you feel there is no place
to go. Whenever you feel lonely, a special angel drops in for
tea. Angels are with you every step of the way and help you
soar with amazing grace. After all, we are angels in training; all we have to do is spread our wings and fly!*

Anonymous

Angels are messengers, but sometimes we misunderstand their language.

Linda Solegato

Angels can fly directly into the heart of the matter.

Anonymous

The soul at its highest is found like God, but an angel gives a closer idea of Him. That is all an angel is: an idea of God.

Meister Eckhart

An angel personifies something new arising from the deep unconscious . . . We can never really know. I simply believe that some part of the human self or soul is not subject to the laws of space and time.

C.S. Jung

Anyone can be an angel, just trust your heart and wing it.

Anonymous

Every man contemplates an angel in his future self.

Ralph Waldo Emerson

Angels: Where They Come From

Make yourself familiar with the angels, and behold them frequently in spirit, for without being seen, angels are present around us.

St Francis de Sales

Whether invoked or not, angels will be present.

Anonymous

We've never had to look far to find our angels. Angels have never really been out of reach. We can always discover angels from the inside out, because it is the angel inside us who can point the way to all our other angels.

Anonymous

It can in no sense be said that heaven is outside of anyone; it is within . . . and a man, also, so far as he receives heaven, is a recipient, a heaven, and an angel.

Emanuel Swedenborg

Angels are all around us all the time, in the very air we breathe.

Eileen Elias Freeman

Millions of spiritual creatures walk the earth unseen,
Unseen, both when we wake and when we sleep.

John Milton

Miracles . . . seem to me to rest not so much upon faces
or voices or healing power coming suddenly near to us
from afar off, but upon our perceptions being made finer,
so that for a moment our eyes can see and our ears can
hear what is there about us always.

Willa Cather

The golden moments in the stream of life rush past us
and we see nothing but sand; the angels come to visit us,
and we only know them when they are gone.

George Eliot

Angels as Guides and Messengers of Comfort, Hope and Inspiration

It's amazing what can truly happen, how your life can be
so grand; when you give up trying on your own, and let
an angel hold your hand.

Anonymous

But if these beings guard you, they do so because they
have been summoned by your prayers.

St Ambrose

We are like children, who stand in need of masters to enlighten us and direct us, and God has provided for this by appointing his angels to be our teachers and our guides.

St Thomas Aquinas

Angels can help us understand what intuition means in a personal way. Angels are actually in charge of a large part of our intuitive self. Viewing intuition from the perspective of angel consciousness, we can say that intuition is our way of tapping into a higher power for guidance and awareness.

Terry Lynn Taylor

When you are lonely or frightened, talk to your guardian angel. You can do it out loud or inside your head – your angel can hear you.

Joan Webster Anderson

Angels don't worry about you . . . They believe in you.

Anonymous

Angels may not come when you call them, but they'll always be there when you need them.

Anonymous

If you seek an angel with an open heart, you shall always find one.

Anonymous

Angels guide us to become spiritual people for the pleasure of it, not for its moralism, because the spiritual life itself has a great deal of beauty and real satisfaction, even pleasure. And this is what the soul needs.

Thomas More

All night, all day, angels watchin' over me, my Lord. All night, all day, angels watchin' over me.

African American spiritual

See, I am sending an angel ahead of you to guard you along the way . . .

Exodus 23: 2

Angels do find us in our hour of need.

Amy Huffman

For every soul, there is a guardian watching it.

The Qur'an

We are never so lost our angels cannot find us.

Stephanie Powers

Beside each man who's born on earth, a guardian angel takes his stand to guide him through life's mysteries.

Menander of Athens

An angel can illuminate the thought and mind of man by strengthening the power of vision.

St Thomas Aquinas

The magnitude of life is overwhelming. Angels are here to help us take it peace by peace.

Levende Waters

Angels assist us in connecting with a powerful yet gentle force, which encourages us to live life to its fullest.

Denise Linn

These things I warmly wish for you – Someone to love, some work to do, A bit o' sun, a bit o' cheer, And a guardian angel always near.

Irish blessing

We Are All Angels to Each Other

But we can all be angels to one another. We can choose to obey the still small stirring within, the little whisper that says, 'Go. Ask. Reach out. Be an answer to someone's plea. You have a part to play. Have faith.' The world will be a better place for it. And wherever they are, the angels will dance.

Joan Webster Anderson

We are each of us angels with only one wing, and we can only fly by embracing one another.

Luciano de Crescenzo

It can in no sense be said that heaven is outside of anyone; it is within . . . and a man, also, as far as he receives heaven, is a recipient, a heaven and an angel.

Emanuel Swedenborg

The pure joy angels feel is like fresh air for the soul. Like a skylight opening, the angel within you can illuminate any circumstance and see everything in a perfect natural light once more. The angel within us is our most basic soul, unfettered.

Karen Goldman

Maybe the tragedy of the human race was that we had forgotten we were each divine.

Shirley MacLaine

If we were all like angels, the world would be a heavenly place.

Anonymous

Seeing and Hearing Angels

Insight is better than eyesight when it comes to seeing an angel.

Eileen Elias Freeman

The guardian angels of life fly so high as to be beyond our sight, but they are always looking down upon us.

Jean Paul Richter

A man on the street is pointing up to the sky. 'Look, an angel,' he yells. Passers-by laugh. 'You fool, that is only a cloud.' How wonderful it would be to see angels where there are only clouds. How sad it would be to see only clouds where there are angels.

Anonymous

Angels are speaking to all of us, all of the time . . . some of us are only listening better.

Anonymous

I believe in angels – they are always hovering near, whispering encouragement whenever clouds appear, protecting us from danger and showing us the way. Performing little miracles within our lives each day.

Anonymous

Holy Angels, our advocates, our brothers, our counsellors, our defenders, our enlighteners, our friends, our guides, our helpers, our intercessors – pray for us.

Mother Teresa of Calcutta

When babies look beyond you and giggle, maybe they're seeing angels.

Eileen Elias Freeman

Whatever you put your attention on in this life will increase in your life. As you put your attention on angels, they will begin increasingly to make their presence known to you.

Denise Linn

I saw them with my bodily eyes as clearly as I see you. And when they departed, I used to weep and wish they would take me with them.

St Joan of Arc

There are moments in our lives, there are moments in a day, when we seem to see beyond the usual – become clairvoyant.

Robert Henri

If trouble hearing Angels' song with thine ears, try listening with thy heart.

Meriel Stelliger

Angels are never too distant to hear you.

Anonymous

When our mortal eyes close on this world for the last time, our angels open our spiritual eyes and escort us personally before the face of God.

Eileen Elias Freeman

If you can't hear the angels, try quieting the static of worry.

Valentine Sterling

If one looks closely enough, one can see angels in every piece of art.

Adeline Cullen Ray

You'll meet more angels on a winding path than on a straight one.

Daisey Verlaef

I saw the angel in the marble and carved until I set him free.

Michelangelo

To see an angel, you must see another's soul.
To feel an angel, you must touch another's heart.
To hear an angel you must listen to both.

Anonymous

When hearts listen, angels sing.

Anonymous

On Earth as It Is in Heaven

Outside the open window
The morning air is all awash with angels.

Richard Purdy Wilbur

Every breath of air and ray of heat and light, every beautiful prospect, is as it were, the skirts of the angel's garments, the waving robes of those whose faces see God.

John Henry Newman

If we could perceive our angels for just a single day, the world would never be the same again, nor would we wish it to be.

Anonymous

All we have to remember is this. Seeing holiness only in others – or only in our own group – is the problem.

Seeing the sacred in ourselves and in all living things is the solution.

Gloria Steinem

Silently, one by one, in the infinite meadows of heaven, Blossomed the lovely stars, the forget-me-nots of the angels.

Henry Wadsworth Longfellow

People see God every day; they just don't recognize him.

Pearl Bailey

Whether invoked or not, angels will be present.

Anonymous

To me every hour of the light and dark is a miracle, Every cubic inch of space is a miracle.

Walt Whitman

If instead of a jewel, or even a flower, we could cast the gift of a lovely thought into the heart of another, that would be giving as the angels must give.

Anonymous

Every raindrop that falls is accompanied by an Angel, for even a raindrop is a manifestation of being.

Mohammed

Music is well said to be the speech of angels.

Thomas Carlyle

Ever felt an angel's breath in the gentle breeze? A teardrop in the falling rain? Hear a whisper amongst the rustle of leaves? Or been kissed by a lone snowflake? Nature is an angel's favourite hiding place.

Carrie Latet

Flowers have spoken to me more than I can tell in written words. They are the hieroglyphics of angels, loved by all men for the beauty of their character, though few can decipher even fragments of their meaning.

Lydia M. Child

Every blade of grass has its angel that bends over it and whispers, 'Grow, grow.'

The Talmud

Legend has it that when someone sobs,
Their tears are caught by butterflies and carried up to heaven.
Angels then float down as teardrops of comfort to take away the sadness.

Anonymous

Perhaps they are not the stars, but rather openings in Heaven where the love of our lost ones pours through and shines down upon us to let us know they are happy.

Eskimo legend

Angels in the Night

Pay attention to your dreams – God's angels often speak directly to our hearts when we are asleep.

Eileen Elias Freeman

Death is not extinguishing the light; it is putting out the lamp because the dawn has come.

Rabindranath Tagore

When someone dies, an angel is there to meet them at the gates of heaven to let them know that their life has just begun.

Anonymous

Death is nothing at all. It does not count. I have only slipped away into the next room. Nothing has happened. Everything remains exactly as it was. I am I, and you are you, and the old life that we lived so fondly together is untouched, unchanged. Whatever we were to each other, that we are still. Call me by the old familiar name. Speak of me in the easy way which you always used. Put no difference into your tone. Wear no forced air of solemnity or sorrow. Laugh as we always laughed at the little jokes that we enjoyed together. Play, smile, think of me, pray for me. Let my name be ever the household word that it always was. Let it be spoken without an effort, without the ghost of a shadow upon it. Life means all that it ever meant. It is the same as it ever was. There is absolute and unbroken continuity. What is this death but a negligible accident? Why should I be out of mind because I am out of sight? I am but waiting for you, for an interval, somewhere very near, just round the corner. All is well.

Henry Scott Holland

The Wonder and Power of Love

How wonderful it must be to speak the language of the angels, with no words for hate and a million words for love!

Eileen Elias Freeman

Angels have no philosophy but love.

Adeline Cullen Ray

Love is how you earn your wings.

Karen Goldman

It is only with the heart that one can see rightly; what is essential is invisible to the eye.

Antoine de Saint-Exupéry

*. . . the angel said, 'I have learned that every man lives,
not through care of himself, but by love.'*

Leo Tolstoy

*The conclusion is always the same: love is the most pow-
erful and still the most unknown energy in the world.*

Pierre Teilhard de Chardin

*To love for the sake of being loved is human, but to love
for the sake of loving is angelic.*

Alphonse de Lamartine

Angel Names

Even though I have never felt the need to name my angels,
I don't have anything against the idea if it helps you
develop a closer, more loving relationship with your
guardian angel. If it is easier for you to build a relationship
with a being whose name you can call on, feel free to ask
your angel to reveal their name or give them a name that
inspires you. Indeed, anything that helps you become more
aware of your angel and more open to their guidance is a
step in the right direction, so if you want to give your
guardian angel a name, rest assured you have their blessing.

When choosing a name steer clear of the minefield of
information about angel names out there and go with a

name you feel comfortable with. Unless you feel it really helps, I wouldn't stress too much choosing the so-called 'right' angel name associated with specific days or months or zodiac signs, just go with what feels right for you. There is no right and wrong with angel names, and if you do settle on a name don't feel it is written in stone. You can change it as often as you like.

If naming your angel feels natural you could go for your own original name, or you could go with the many 'named' angels. If you'd like to start with a 'named' angel the list below is by no means definitive, as there are literally thousands of angel names worldwide, but it includes some of the popular 'named' angels gathered from religion, mythology and lore. As you look through the list be aware of any sensations you experience while reading a particular name – any resonance could be an invitation by your guardian angel to connect with you more deeply.

Ambriel – angel of truth and protection
Ariel – angel protector of nature, pets, birds and animals
Auriel – angel name meaning 'light of God'
Azrael – angel of grief and dying
Balthial – angel of peace and contentment, can help you overcome feelings of jealousy

Barbiel – angel of good fortune and success

Camael – angel of beauty and joy on the outside and on the inside

Cathetel – angel protector of the garden, fruits and vegetables

Chamuel – this angel fosters tolerance in the human heart, inspiring within us the realization that to love others we must love ourselves

Duma – the angel of silence

Elemeniah – angel protector of those at sea or on the water

Gabriel – high-ranking angel of love and gratitude

Haniel – angel whose name means 'glory of God'

Harahel – angel protector of those who seek knowledge

Jeremiel – angel whose name means 'mercy of God'

Jophiel – angel of creativity and spirituality

Liwet – angel of love and original thought and invention

Metatron – angel of careers, relationships and spiritual gifts

Michael – high-ranking angel of virtue, power and protection

Mihr – angel of friendship and companionship

Nemamiah – angel protector of those who fight for the cause of justice

Raguel – angel of harmony, fairness and justice

Raphael – high-ranking angel of healing and truth

Raziel – angel of secret wisdom and mysteries

Rhamiel – angel of compassion and mercy

Samandiriel – angel of creativity and imagination

Sandalphon – angel who is especially receptive to prayers

Sariel – angel of healing

Seheiah – angel of protection against sickness

Uriel – high-ranking angel of transformation, devotion and peace

Zadkiel – angel of forgiveness, comfort and guidance

If You Prefer to Connect with Angels Associated with Specific Life Problems You Could Choose from the Following:

Childbirth and childcare – Raphael and Sandalphon

Confidence – Sandalphon and Zadkiel

Communications – Gabriel

Creativity – Gabriel

Disagreements – Ariel and Gabriel

Financial problems – Michael

Fixing problems – Michael

Gardening and the environment – Uriel

Grief and dying – Azrael and Raphael

Healing and health – Raphael and Metatron

Homes and lost objects – Chamuel

Insomnia – Michael

Learning and studying – Harabel and Uriel

Memory – Zadkiel

Overcoming obstacles – Raphael

Protection – Chamuel

Psychic development – Jeremiel

Relationships and love – Haniel

Spiritual development – Metatron and Sandalphon

Travelling – Raphael

World peace – Chamuel

And If You Need a Specific Angel to Help with a Day of the Week or Time of Year You Could Choose One of the Following:

Angels of the week

Monday – Gabriel

Tuesday – Camael

Wednesday – Michael

Thursday – Zadkiel

Friday – Haniel

Saturday – Tzaphiel

Sunday – Raphael

Angels of the seasons

Spring – Raphael

Summer – Ariel

Autumn – Michael

Winter – Gabriel

There Are Also Angels That Watch over Each Birth Sign:

Aries – Machidiel (angel of March) and Uriel

Taurus – Asmodel (angel of April) and Michael

Gemini – Ambriel (angel of May) and Uriel

Cancer – Muriel (angel of June) and Gabriel

Leo – Verchief (angel of July) and Raphael

Virgo – Hamaliel (angel of August) and Michael

Libra – Zuriel (angel of September) and Uriel

Scorpio – Barbiel (angel of October) and Gabriel

Sagittarius – Adnachiel (angel of November) and Raphael

Capricorn – Hanael (angel of December) and Michael

Aquarius – Cambiel (angel of January) and Uriel

Pisces – Barchiel (angel of February) and Gabriel

Bear in mind with all these lists of specific angel names that different sources may list different angels for specific days or problems. Angel names come from a huge variety of sources, religious texts, magical references and folklore and some angels have different names or the same name spelled in a different way according to which part of the world or which source is being referenced. And some references indicate that the names do not belong to individual angels at all, but instead refer to whole hosts of angels. Again, I want to stress that there is no right or wrong and no definitive 'angel name' list.

If you don't feel drawn to any of the names on this list or any other angel names you have found in books or on the Internet that's not a problem. Despite there being lots of information about angel names, it is not a science and, as mentioned earlier, angels don't really have names at all. You can simply choose a name that inspires respect or feelings of comfort and joy. It is important to go with what works best for you, a name that you love.

We are human beings, after all, and many of us like to have names for everything in our lives, angels included. If chosen carefully and used wisely, there is a special magic in names, something to associate with, so if you want to call your guardian angel a name or a nickname – whether or not that name is their actual name – go ahead, make it official, and name your guardian angel.

Angelic Poetry

Poems about angels are precious creations and I've enclosed a few of my favourites below. You'll notice that some of the authors are very well known, others are anonymous but well known and others are by unknown poets you may not have heard of (yet) because they were sent to me by readers. I'm placing them all together to underline that angels are for everyone and you don't need to be a literary genius to write moving poetry or inspiring words about them. There is a deep well of creativity within every one of us and we can all become artists and poets if we leave our hearts and our imagination open. Indeed, nothing gives your angels more joy than you using your creativity to write about them – or if writing isn't your thing when you draw, paint, sculpt, compose, write, sing or dance with them in mind – because creativity is spirit, a place where truth and beauty can meet.

'Touched By an Angel' by Maya Angelou

We, unaccustomed to courage
exiles from delight
live coiled in shells of loneliness
until love leaves its high holy temple
and comes into our sight
to liberate us into life.

Love arrives
and in its train come ecstasies
old memories of pleasure
ancient histories of pain.
Yet if we are bold,
love strikes away the chains of fear
from our souls.

We are weaned from our timidity
In the flush of love's light
we dare be brave
And suddenly we see
that love costs all we are
and will ever be.
Yet it is only love
which sets us free.

'Air and Angels' by John Donne

This is perhaps the most famous angel poem in the English language so I want to include it here. Don't worry if you struggle to understand it. I'm still not quite sure what it means. It seems that Donne is comparing the purity of angels with the purity and subtlety of air, something we, of course, can't live without, but perhaps the best way to understand it is to stop trying to understand and simply say the words out loud and let them flow into your heart and soul.

Twice or thrice had I loved thee,
Before I knew thy face or name;
So in a voice, so in a shapeless flame
Angels affect us oft, and worshipp'd be.
Still when, to where thou wert, I came,
Some lovely glorious nothing did I see.

But since my soul, whose child love is,
Takes limbs of flesh, and else could nothing do,
More subtle than the parent is
Love must not be, but take a body too;
And therefore what thou wert, and who,
I bid Love ask, and now
That it assume thy body, I allow,
And fix itself in thy lip, eye, and brow.

Whilst thus to ballast love I thought,
And so more steadily to have gone,
With wares which would sink admiration,
I saw I had love's pinnace overfraught;
Thy every hair for love to work upon
Is much too much; some fitter must be sought;
For, nor in nothing, nor in things
Extreme, and scattering bright, can love inhere;
Then as an angel face and wings
Of air, not pure as it, yet pure doth wear,
So thy love may be my love's sphere;
Just such disparity
As is 'twixt air's and angels' purity,
'Twixt women's love, and men's, will ever be.

'A Dying Child' by Hans Christian Andersen

(I always feel this poem should be called 'A Living Child')

Mother, I'm so tired, I want to sleep now;
Let me fall asleep and feel you near
Please don't cry – there now, you'll promise, won't you?
On my face I felt your burning tear,
Here's so cold and winds outside are frightening,
But in dreams – ah, that's what I like best;
I can see the darling angel children
When I shut my sleepy eyes and rest.
Mother, look, the angel's here beside me!
Listen, too, how sweet the music grows.
See, his wings are both so white and lovely;
Surely it was God who gave him those.
Green and red and yellow floating round me,
They are flowers the angel came and spread.
Shall I, too, have wings while I'm alive, or –
Mother, is it only when I'm dead?
Why do you take hold of me so tightly,
Put your cheek to mine the way you do?
And your cheek is wet, but yet it's burning –
Mother I shall always be with you . . .
Yes, but then you mustn't go on sighing;
When you cry I cry as well, you see.
I'm so tired – my eyes they won't stay open –
Mother – look – the Angel's kissing me!

'Do Not Stand at My Grave and Weep'
by Mary Frye

You've probably heard this poem read out at funerals. If I had my way it would be a compulsory reading at all funerals, because it remains one of the most simple but powerful expressions of comfort for those grieving the loss of a loved one.

Do not stand at my grave and weep
I am not there, I do not sleep.
I am a thousand winds that blow
I am the diamond glint on snow.
I am the sunlight on ripened grain
I am the gentle autumn rain.
When you wake in the morning hush
I am the swift uplifting rush
Of quiet birds in circling flight
I am the soft stars that shine at night.
Do not stand at my grave and cry
I am not there, I did not die.

'Heart Prints' by an Unknown Author

Whatever our hands touch –
We leave fingerprints!
On walls, on furniture
On doorknobs, dishes, books.
There's no escape.
As we touch we leave our identity.

Wherever I go today
Help me leave heartprints!
Heartprints of compassion
Of understanding and love.
Heartprints of kindness
And genuine concern.

May my heart touch a lonely neighbour
Or a runaway daughter
Or an anxious mother
Or perhaps an aged grandfather.

Send me out today
To leave heartprints.
And if someone should say,
'I felt your touch,'
May they also sense the love
that is deep within my heart.

'Angel Blessing' by an Unknown Author

Angels around us, angels beside us, angels within us. Angels are watching over you when times are good or stressed. Their wings wrap gently around you, whispering you are loved and blessed.

'Life is a Miracle' by an Unknown Author

Life is a miracle . . . don't let it slip away,
Open your heart to others . . . give of yourself each day.
See the beauty in everyone, regardless of where they've
*   been,*
Some have a difficult journey and really need a friend.
Share your gifts and talents . . . listen with your heart.
Do the things you dream about but don't have time to
*   start.*
Pick a bouquet of flowers . . . show someone that you
*   care,*
Be gracious and forgiving . . . life is not always fair.
Hold on to your courage . . . you may need it down the
*   road,*
We all have a cross to bear . . . it could be a heavy load.
If you practise all these things no matter where you
*   roam,*
You may find both sun and rain but you'll never feel
*   alone.*

'Guardian Angel Feather' by an Unknown Author

This is an angel feather,
sent from God above,
to serve as a reminder,
of his gracious love.
It's from your guardian angel,
that God himself assigned to you,
And fell out in his struggles,
as he protected you.

Each time you almost stumble,
Each time you nearly fall,
Remember to
Thank God and his angels,
for answering your call.

'My Guardian Angel' (Psalm 91: 11–12)

Dear Angel ever at my side, how lovely you must be –
To leave your home in heaven,
to guard a child like me.
When I'm far away from home,
or maybe hard at play –
I know you will protect me,
from harm along the way.
Your beautiful and shining face,

I see not, though you're near.
The sweetness of your lovely voice,
I cannot really hear.
When I pray, you're praying too,
Your prayer is just for me.
But, when I sleep you never do,
You're watching over me.

'An Angel's Touch' by Gareth Simon Gameson

A hand upon your shoulder
That gives you comfort and solace
A loving kiss upon your cheek
That puts a smile upon your face
A tender hand in your hand
So that you won't feel alone
Are signs from your Guardian Angel
That you are never on your own

'White Feathers' by Sue Gulliver

Have you ever seen a white feather lying in your path?
And wondered, 'where did that come from?' and wryly
    laugh?
Did you think that a bird had dropped it or did you get
    a shiver?
Or did you think an archer had lost it from his quiver?

Just think when you next see a white feather on the
*   ground,*
Am I being silly or has my Guardian Angel been
*   around?*
If you've needed guidance or help in anyway,
Has your problem been solved or eased at the end of the
*   day?*

I believe in Angels and ask them all the time,
To help me, my friends and family through the daily
*   grind.*
They are around you to give guidance and help you all
*   they can,*
So don't be afraid to ask them, cos they've been sent by
*   The Main Man.*

'Your Guardian Angel' by an Unknown Author

You have a Guardian Angel
Who watches over you –
Everywhere you go
And everything you do.

This gentle, silent helper
Is there to be your guide
To shelter and protect you,
And for you to walk beside.

Your Angel will always help you
Whenever things go wrong,
They'll be the wings beneath your feet
As Life's path you walk along.

Feel this calming presence –
Be enfolded by its love
And let your life be guided
By a power from above.

Angels can inspire us to express ourselves creatively. If your words or work feel disjointed or awkward at first, don't give up. Keep practising and with the help of your angels you will get there. The secret to creativity is passion – you have to *want* to do it. And when you have created something unique, share it with others, or send it my way. I'd love to read it and share it with a wider audience because each time a gift shares hands, an angel is born.

Angel Voices

This section is a selection of stories and insights sent to me by readers with a common theme and that is to show how, although the voices of angels can come to us in many ways, perhaps the most powerful way is when that voice comes from *within*. The voices of love, goodness and hope are always within us and the more we listen to them the more we can hear them and be guided and transformed by them.

It is, of course, possible to live without angels in much the same way as you can live without love or music, poetry or art. But such a life is an impoverished one because on a very deep level we need to connect to the divine within and around us. As reflections of our own creativity and divine potential, angels speak to the deepest and best part of ourselves and so this final part of the book is dedicated to the aspiring angel inside you, the part of you that you can never love enough because, in truth, it is who you really are.

The Little Girl in the Park

I am indebted to Clare for sending me this wonderful story. It is an allegory rather than a true life story, but it never fails to inspire me.

There was this little girl one day sitting in the park. Everyone passed and never stopped to see why she looked so sad. Dressed in a worn pink dress, barefoot and dirty, the girl just sat and watched the people go by. She never tried to speak, she never said a word.

Many people passed, but not one person stopped. Just so happens the next day I decided to go back to the park, in curiosity, to see if the little girl would still be there. Right in the very spot as yesterday she sat perched on high, with the saddest look in her eyes. Today I was to make my own move and walk over to the little girl. For as we all know a park full of strange people is not a place for young children to play alone. As I got closer I could see the girl's back was hunched with deformity. I figured that was a reason the people just passed by and made no effort to help.

Having a deformity was a big blow in our society and, 'so heaven help you' if you make a step towards assisting someone who is different. As I got closer, the little girl slightly lowered her eyes to avoid my intent stare. As I approached her, I could see the shape of her back more clearly. Grotesquely shaped in a humped-over form. I smiled to let her know it was OK, I was there to help, to talk. I sat down beside her and opened with a simple 'Hello'.

The little girl acted shocked and stammered a 'Hi' after a long stare into my eyes. I smiled and she shyly smiled back.

We talked till darkness fell and the park was completely empty. Everyone was gone and we were alone. I asked the girl why she was so sad. The little girl looked at me and with a sad face said, 'Because I'm different.'

I immediately said, 'That you are!' and smiled.

The little girl acted even sadder, she said, 'I know.'

'Little girl,' I said, 'you remind me of an angel, sweet and innocent.'

She looked at me and smiled, slowly she got to her feet and said, 'Really?'

'Yes, ma'am, you're like a little guardian angel sent to watch over all those people walking by.'

She nodded her head yes and smiled, with that she spread her wings and said, 'I'm your guardian angel,' with a twinkle in her eye. I was speechless . . . sure I was seeing things. She said, 'For once you thought of someone other than yourself, my job here is done.'

I jumped to my feet and said, 'Wait, so why did no one stop to help an angel?'

She looked at me and smiled, 'You're the only one that could see me, you believe, it's in your heart.'

And she was gone. And with that my life was changed dramatically. So, when you think you're all you have, remember, your angel is always watching over you.

Italy Island

This story was submitted to a *Sunday Post* reader's page and sent to me by Charlotte. Again it reminds us that we can all be angels to each other.

While visiting the church on Italy Island I came across some children leaving notes on the board for loved ones who had passed on. A little girl asked me to pin her note up because she couldn't reach. She said thank you and explained the note was for her daddy.

'It's my birthday soon,' she explained, 'and he said he would buy me a special baby doll, but we've moved to a new house so I've sent him my new address.'

When she left the church I could not resist having a peep at her note and making a note of her birthday and her address. I bought her the sweetest doll I could find and sent it with a note explaining that because there were no shops in heaven I have done your daddy's shopping for him.

I signed my letter from the lady who pinned your note on the board in the church on Italy Island.

The Window

This enlightening story, doing the rounds on the Internet, was sent to me by Cheryl.

Two men, both seriously ill, occupied the same hospital room. One man was allowed to sit up in his bed for an hour a day to drain the fluids from his lungs. His bed was next to the room's only window. The other man had to spend all his time flat on his back.

The men talked for hours on end. They spoke of their wives and families, their homes, their jobs, their involvement in the military service, where they had been on vacation. And every afternoon when the man in the bed next to the window could sit up, he would pass the time by describing to his roommate all the things he could see outside the window.

The man in the other bed would live for those one-hour periods where his world would be broadened and enlivened by all the activity and colour of the outside world. The window overlooked a park with a lovely lake, the man had said. Ducks and swans played on the water while children sailed their model boats. Lovers walked arm in arm amid flowers of every colour of the rainbow. Grand old trees graced the landscape, and a fine view of the city skyline could be seen in the distance. As the man by the window described all this in exquisite detail, the man on the other side of the room would close his eyes and imagine the picturesque scene.

One warm afternoon the man by the window described a parade passing by. Although the other man could not hear the band, he could see it in his mind's eye as the gentleman by the window portrayed it with descriptive words. Unexpectedly, an alien thought entered his head: Why should he have all the pleasure of seeing everything while I never get to see anything? It didn't seem fair. As the thought fermented, the man felt ashamed at first. But as the days passed and he missed seeing more sights, his envy eroded into resentment and soon turned him sour. He began to brood and found himself unable to sleep. He should be by that window – and that thought now controlled his life.

Late one night, as he lay staring at the ceiling, the man by the window began to cough. He was choking on the fluid in his lungs. The other man watched in the dimly lit room as the struggling man by the window groped for the button to call for help. Listening from across the room, he never moved, never pushed his own button which would have brought the nurse running. In less than five minutes, the coughing and choking stopped, along with the sound of breathing. Now, there was only silence – deathly silence.

The following morning, the day nurse arrived to bring water for their baths. When she found the lifeless body of the man by the window, she was saddened and called the hospital attendant to take it away – no words, no fuss. As soon as it seemed appropriate, the man asked if he could be moved next to the window. The nurse was happy to make the switch and after making sure he was comfortable, she left him alone.

Slowly, painfully, he propped himself up on one elbow to take his first look. Finally, he would have the joy of seeing it all himself. He strained slowly to turn to look out of the window beside the bed. It faced a blank wall.

Putting the 'I' into Love

We're probably all familiar with the famous verses from 1 Corinthians 13: 4–7 because they are so often used for wedding vows:

> Love is patient, love is kind. It does not envy, it does not boast, it is not proud. It is not rude, it is not self-seeking, it is not easily angered, it keeps no record of wrongs. Love does not delight in evil but rejoices with the truth. It always protects, always trusts, always hopes, always perseveres.

But how much more personal and relevant these verses become if we substitute 'I' for the word love?

> I am patient, I am kind. I do not envy, I do not boast, I am not proud. I am not rude, I am not self-seeking, I am not easily angered, I keep no record of wrongs. I do not delight in evil but rejoice in the truth. I always protect, always trust, always hope, always persevere.

And to take things even higher – from the angels within to the angels all around us:

> Angels are patient, angels are kind. They do not envy, they do not boast, they are not proud. They are not rude,

they are not self-seeking, they are not easily angered, they keep no record of wrongs. Angels do not delight in evil but rejoice in the truth. They always protect, always trust, always hope, always persevere.

Don't We All?

This story never fails to grab my attention. It was sent to me three years ago by Greg and I often find myself revisiting it.

I was parked in front of the mall wiping off my car. I had just come from the car wash and was waiting for my wife to get out of work. Coming my way from across the car park was what society would consider a bum. From the looks of him, he had no car, no home, no clean clothes, and no money. There are times when you feel generous but there are other times that you just don't want to be bothered. This was one of those 'don't want to be bothered times'.

'I hope he doesn't ask me for any money,' I thought. He didn't. He came and sat on the kerb in front of the bus stop but he didn't look like he could have enough money to even ride the bus. After a few minutes he spoke.

'That's a very pretty car,' he said.

He was ragged but he had an air of dignity about him. His scraggly blond beard kept more than his face warm. I said 'Thanks' and continued wiping off my car.

He sat there quietly as I worked. The expected plea for money never came. As the silence between us widened something inside said, 'Ask him if he needs any help.' I was sure that he would say 'Yes' but I held true to the inner voice.

'Do you need any help?' I asked.

He answered in three simple but profound words that I shall never forget. We often look for wisdom in great men and women. We expect it from those of higher learning and accomplishments. I expected nothing but an outstretched grimy hand. He spoke the three words that shook me.

'Don't we all?' he said.

I was feeling high and mighty, successful and important, above a bum in the street, until those three words hit me like a twelve-gauge shotgun. Don't we all? I needed help. Maybe not for bus fare or a place to sleep, but I needed help. I reached in my wallet and gave him not only enough for bus fare, but enough to get a warm meal and shelter for the day. Those three little words still ring true. No matter how much you have, no matter how much you have accomplished, you need help too. No matter how little you have, no matter how loaded you are with problems, even without money or a place to sleep, you can give help.

Even if it's just a compliment, you can give that. You never know when you may see someone that appears to *have it all. They are waiting on you to give them what they don't have. A different perspective on life, a glimpse at something beautiful, a respite from daily chaos, that only you through a torn world can see. Maybe the man was just a homeless stranger wandering the streets. Maybe he was more than that. Maybe he was sent by a power that is great and wise, to minister to a soul too comfortable in themselves.*

Maybe God looked down, called an Angel, dressed him like a bum, then said, 'Go minister to that man cleaning the car, that man needs help.' Don't we all?

The Little Boy in the Street

And to finish is this short but precious angel story, which I feel sums up this section of the book better than I ever could:

On the street I saw a little boy cold and shivering in a thin pair of shorts and a threadbare shirt. I got angry and asked my angels, 'Why did you permit this? Why don't you do something about it?'

My angel replied, 'I certainly did do something about it – I brought you here.'

All these inspiring stories are powerful reminders that angels don't just exist outside ourselves – they also exist in each one of us. If you don't feel angels working in your life one of the best ways to discover them is from the inside out. You may not realize it but everything you say and do can touch those around you in a divine way. Just feeling love or compassion for others is angelic. A kind word can help someone see the goodness around them; an act of kindness can bring beauty into another person's life and restore their faith in human nature and in themselves.

Whenever you reveal your inner angel, you remind others of the divine potential within them. You become the message and the inspiration because others see something remarkable, something angelic, in you. It goes straight past their egos and quietly sneaks in through the back door of their hearts. Then, in time, it will knock from within and awaken them, just as it has awakened you.

Good Day to You and Your Companion

Centuries ago in France peasants had a wonderful tradition. They didn't say 'hello' when they met each other. Instead they would say, 'Good day to you and your companion.' Although they couldn't see them, they thought that a person's guardian angel needed to be greeted too.

I hope that reading this book has encouraged you to be more open to the possibility that even though you can't always see, hear, feel or touch it something wonderful exists within and around you. The big issue is: can you open your mind and heart to the wonder? Can you be open to the possibility that your guardian angel is walking beside you? Can you let your guardian angel guide, heal and inspire you?

As always when I write, I never fail to be moved by the eloquence of the words people use to talk about angels, and by their need to express or give voice to the divine. Today, just as they have always been, angels are everywhere. Crossing barriers of time, religion, geography and language they are awakening our thoughts, dreams and hopes. They are, and always will be, the divine caretakers of our souls, our world and our universe and, if you sincerely want to, you can find your guardian angel and experience all the love, happiness and magic the world of spirit can bring to everything and anyone, however ordinary and mundane. There is nothing stopping you from seeing your divine helpers. Your angels have not been hiding from you. You may just have been hiding from them.

However difficult the journey of your life becomes never forget that celestial helpers are always by your side, listening and waiting for you to reach out and greet them through the window of your creativity and the open door of your heart. The more you become aware of the angels that exist within and all around you the greater the possibility of receiving their guidance and inspiration.

And once you find this volcano of truth and hope within you, not only will you be uplifted to the dance and the magic of everything good in this life and the next, you will also be able to say with absolute joy and certainty, 'Now, I *can* see angels.'

Calling All Angels

Finally, if at any point while reading this book you felt puzzled, or you have a story or insight you want to share, or a burning question you need answered or want to discuss further, don't hesitate to get in touch with me. Please don't feel you are alone in all this. I welcome all your angel stories, thoughts and questions. You can contact me care of Simon and Schuster, 1st Floor, 222 Gray's Inn Road, London, WC1X 8HB, or email me direct at angeltalk710@aol.com. I'd be happy to hear from you, and with the loving guidance of my angels will try to answer every single question and story personally; communicating with you is the thing I love most about writing angel books.

Further Reading

Angels in the Early Modern World, A. Walsham and P. Marshall, Cambridge University Press, 2006.

The Case for Angels, Peter Williams, Paternoster, Carlisle, 2002.

Angels, Jane Williams, Lion Publishing, Oxford, 2006.

Angels: A History, David Jones, Oxford University Press, 2010.

Seeing Angels, Emma Heathcote-Jones, John Blake, London, 2002.

The Physics of Angels: Exploring the Realm Where Science and Angels Meet, Rupert Sheldrake and Matthew Fox, Harper, San Francisco, 1996.

Note on the Author

Theresa Cheung is the author of a variety of books including the *Sunday Times* best-selling *An Angel Called My Name: Inspiring True Stories from the Other Side*, *An Angel On My Shoulder: Incredible True Stories from the Other Side* and *Angel Babies: And Other Amazing True Stories of Guardian Angels*. She is also the author of the international best-seller *The Element Encyclopedia of 20,000 Dreams*, and *The Element Encyclopedia of the Psychic World* and the recent top 10 *Sunday Times* best-seller *An Angel Healed Me: True Stories of Heavenly Encounters*. Her books have been translated into twenty different languages and her writing has featured in *It's Fate*, *Spirit & Destiny* and *Prediction* magazines. In addition, Theresa has worked on books for Derek Acorah, Yvette Fielding, Tony Stockwell and Dr William Bloom. Born into a family of psychics and spiritualists she has been involved in the research of psychic phenomena for over twenty-five years since gaining a Masters degree from King's College, Cambridge. She has also been a student at the College of Psychic Studies in London.